Mata Hari and Other Plays

Seven Plays by
Don Nigro

A Samuel French Acting Edition

Founded 1830

SAMUELFRENCH.COM
SAMUELFRENCH-LONDON.CO.UK

Copyright © 2013, 2015 by Don Nigro
All Rights Reserved
Cover Model: Tatyana Kot
Photographer: Romi Burianova

MATA HARI AND OTHER PLAYS is fully protected under the copyright laws of the United States of America, the British Commonwealth, including Canada, and all other countries of the Copyright Union. All rights, including professional and amateur stage productions, recitation, lecturing, public reading, motion picture, radio broadcasting, television and the rights of translation into foreign languages are strictly reserved.

ISBN 978-0-573-79988-4

www.SamuelFrench.com
www.SamuelFrench-London.co.uk

For Production Enquiries

United States and Canada
Info@SamuelFrench.com
1-866-598-8449

United Kingdom and Europe
Plays@SamuelFrench-London.co.uk
020-7255-4302

Each title is subject to availability from Samuel French, depending upon country of performance. Please be aware that *MATA HARI AND OTHER PLAYS* may not be licensed by Samuel French in your territory. Professional and amateur producers should contact the nearest Samuel French office or licensing partner to verify availability.

CAUTION: Professional and amateur producers are hereby warned that *MATA HARI AND OTHER PLAYS* is subject to a licensing fee. Publication of this play(s) does not imply availability for performance. Both amateurs and professionals considering a production are strongly advised to apply to Samuel French before starting rehearsals, advertising, or booking a theatre. A licensing fee must be paid whether the title(s) is presented for charity or gain and whether or not admission is charged. Professional/Stock licensing fees are quoted upon application to Samuel French.

No one shall make any changes in this title(s) for the purpose of production. No part of this book may be reproduced, stored in a retrieval system, or transmitted in any form, by any means, now known or yet to be invented, including mechanical, electronic, photocopying, recording, videotaping, or otherwise, without the prior written permission of the publisher. No one shall upload this title(s), or part of this title(s), to any social media websites.

For all enquiries regarding motion picture, television, and other media rights, please contact Samuel French.

MUSIC USE NOTE

Licensees are solely responsible for obtaining formal written permission from copyright owners to use copyrighted music in the performance of this play and are strongly cautioned to do so. If no such permission is obtained by the licensee, then the licensee must use only original music that the licensee owns and controls. Licensees are solely responsible and liable for all music clearances and shall indemnify the copyright owners of the play(s) and their licensing agent, Samuel French, against any costs, expenses, losses and liabilities arising from the use of music by licensees. Please contact the appropriate music licensing authority in your territory for the rights to any incidental music.

IMPORTANT BILLING AND CREDIT REQUIREMENTS

If you have obtained performance rights to this title, please refer to your licensing agreement for important billing and credit requirements.

CONTENTS

Mata Hari 5

Marina. 35

Queens 65

The Wood Where Things Have No Names. 71

Pentecost. 77

Lamp Post 91

Zombie Radio 107

Mata Hari

For Tatyana Kot

MATA HARI was first presented along with Marina on June 15, 2013 at the Robert Moss Theatre, 440 Lafayette Street, New York City, by Nylon Fusion Theatre Company as part of the Planet Connections Theatre Festivity, with the following cast:

MATA HARI . . . . Tatyana Kot
MACLEOD . . . . Curtis James Nielsen

Directed by Ivette Dumeng

The rest of the creative team was:

Scenic Designer . . . . Tijana Bjelajac
Sound Designer . . . . Andy Evan Cohen
Costume Designer . . . . Hope Governali
Lighting Designer . . . . Dan Stearns
Choreography . . . . Natasa Trifan
Stage Manager . . . . Laura Malseed
Publicist . . . . Bunch of People
Assistant Stage Manager . . . . Kimberly Flores
Graphic Design and Property Master. . . . . Greg Kanyicska
Doll Designer. . . . . Juliana Francis Kelly
House Manager . . . . Juan Garcia
Cover Photography . . . . Graeme Malcolm (Mata Hari),
Theik Smith (Marina)

CHARACTERS

MATA HARI – early forties
MACLEOD – early sixties

SETTING & TIME

The jail cell of Mata Hari in the year 1917. Night.

AN IMPORTANT NOTE ON SAFETY

Under no circumstances should blanks be used in any performance of this play. The gunshot sounds, including the pistol shot, must be sounds made offstage only. Any use of blanks or any other devices which could harm the performers will result in immediate withdrawal of permission to produce this play.

(In the darkness, the sounds of insects in the jungle, and an Indonesian gamelan playing softly. Lights up on **MATA HARI**, *wearing a fairly simple and modest dark dress. She is past forty and beautiful, but months in prison have taken a toll on her.)*

MATA HARI. Sometimes I dream of the Indies. It's pleasant to sit on the verandah in the dry season, but when the rains come, everything is damp. There is mold creeping up the walls, and everything rots. Not unlike this place. In this place the beds are full of vermin, and there are rats everywhere. At first I was terrified of the rats. They disgusted me, and I hated them. But as the days blur one into another I've gotten used to them, even become rather fond of them. They're survivors, like me. I can respect that. Some of these rats possess deeper and more complex souls than many individuals I have encountered in the French judicial system. Look at my judges. Look at that row of pathetic, stern faced, smelly old hypocrites. They look like they've just crawled down off the pictures on cigar boxes. Half of them want to make love to me and the other half think they already have. And they're intercepting my letters. All I want to do is communicate with Vadime. My beautiful Russian lover thinks I've forgotten him. How stupid I was to imagine that any man ever really cared for me. How quickly they abandon me. How cravenly they scuttle away. Not one of them has a rat's testicle's worth of courage. And my poor Russian boy is risking his life at the front for the French government which is determined to kill me. Dearest Marina, he called me. I can't think of him without weeping. What gives them the right to intercept my correspondence? What have I done to make you treat me this way? I have been beautiful, I have given men pleasure, I have danced, and this is my reward.

(Sound of a cell door creaking open in the darkness.)

What's that? Is somebody here? Have you brought me something to eat? Have you pardoned me, finally? Am I to be saved after all? Hello? Who's there?

MACLEOD. *(Stepping into the light, a man in his sixties, with a large black satchel.)* Who do you think it is? God? Would God waste his time on a slut like you?

MATA HARI. What are you doing here?

MACLEOD. You don't seem very happy to see me. That was not always the case. There was a time when you'd have got down on your knees and thanked God to see me. But then, you've spent more time on your knees than a scrubwoman.

MATA HARI. How did you get in here? I can't believe they actually let you in. They haven't been letting anybody in to see me.

MACLEOD. I'm your husband. I have a right to see my wife, even if she is a traitor and a prostitute.

MATA HARI. Don't call me that.

MACLEOD. Don't call you which? Traitor, or prostitute? Which do you find more offensive? The treason is a slightly more recent development, of course. At least on the international scale. You were a whore when I married you. I was just too befuddled with lust to see it.

MATA HARI. I haven't committed any sort of treason, and I was not a whore. I was hardly more than a child. And you were old and mean to me. But I don't want to argue with you. I want out of this place. Can you help me get out of here?

MACLEOD. Nobody forced you to marry me. Nobody forced you to answer my advertisement. And look what I got.

MATA HARI. Well, what did you expect? What kind of a man advertises for a wife in the newspapers?

MACLEOD. What kind of woman answers?

MATA HARI. A poor, innocent one. Someone you knew you could take advantage of.

MACLEOD. I took advantage of you? What a joke that is. You were never innocent. You were always conniving. Always a flirt. All the men were always gaping at you.

MATA HARI. And what was I supposed to do about that? If you wanted an ugly wife you should have made it clear in the advertisement. You were lucky to get me. And all the time we were married you were sleeping with other women.

MACLEOD. A husband's private life is none of the wife's business. I rescued you from a ditch but you crawled right back in the gutter the first chance you got.

MATA HARI. You tried to pimp me out to your friends to pay for your gambling debts. And you gave me syphilis. Was that also not my business?

MACLEOD. Maybe somebody gave you syphilis, but don't blame me. For all I know, you gave ME syphilis. God knows how many men you've slept with. It would take the rest of your life just to make a list.

MATA HARI. It's not that many. Vadime de Massloff, who is my true love. Xavier Rousseau. Henri de Rothschild. The Marquis de Beaufort. Baron de Roland. The Marquis de Paladines. Lieutenant Baerveldt. Levinus T. Keuchenis. The Sultan of Atjeh. Count Carlo Marenco. Christian de Mouchy. Natalie Barney.

MACLEOD. Good Christ.

MATA HARI. I learned quite a bit from her. Otto Bunge. Captain Kuntze. No, wait. Runtze. Not Kuntze. Was it Runtze or Kuntze? Hendrickus something. Prince di San Faustino. Sir Basil Thompson. Piet van der Hem. Karel van der Heyden. The headmaster of my girls' school.

MACLEOD. All right. That's enough.

MATA HARI. Captain Van Mourik. The Dutch Consul in Madrid. Ferdinand van Bissing. Crown Prince Wilhelm.

Captain Hoffmann. The other Captain Hoffmann. The Cross Eyed Captain Hoffman. An old Dutchman with an ear trumpet.

MACLEOD. I really don't care.

MATA HARI. The Uruguayan Consul in Paris. He had a really big one. Two teenage boys in the Hague. Henri Kapferret, the daredevil pilot. He flew over Paris upside down.

MACLEOD. Stop it.

MATA HARI. And we did it upside down. Although not in the airplane. Well, we did it in the airplane, but not upside down. He was afraid we'd fall out.

MACLEOD. What a tragedy that would have been.

MATA HARI. We did it sideways in his dirigible. If you've never had intercourse in a Zeppelin, you really should try it.

MACLEOD. I don't want to have intercourse in a Zeppelin. Now would you please –

MATA HARI. Wait. I'm not done yet. Christoph Gluck. The Duke of Cumberland's brother. The Duke of Cumberland. Sneek van Hoogslop. Peter van Boom.

MACLEOD. FOR GOD'S SAKE WILL YOU JUST SHUT UP ABOUT YOUR DAMNED LOVERS?

MATA HARI. Well, fine. Don't ask a question if you don't want to know the answer.

MACLEOD. I didn't ask a question. And I don't give a shit how many men you've slept with. I just don't want to stand here and listen to you enumerate them until Doomsday.

MATA HARI. Do you know what I think?

MACLEOD. I never know what you think. You've never had a coherent thought in your life.

MATA HARI. I think you still care for me.

MACLEOD. I couldn't possibly care less about you.

MATA HARI. Somewhere deep inside you do.

MACLEOD. I have nothing deep inside. And if I ever did, you killed it a long time ago.

MATA HARI. No, it's still there. That's why you've come here. I can tell about these things. Trust me.

MACLEOD. I don't trust you any farther than I could drop kick you.

MATA HARI. I only flirted with other men to make you jealous. You like being jealous. You can only get excited when you're in a jealous rage.

MACLEOD. That's a lie. I am always absolutely under control.

MATA HARI. Were you under control when you called me horrible names, spat on me, bit me, and beat me with a buggy whip?

MACLEOD. I never beat you with a buggy whip. It was a cat-o-nine-tails. And you deserved it. You were having intimate relations with half the men on the island of Java.

MATA HARI. Because my husband didn't want me. You had a beautiful wife, young enough to be your daughter, and you didn't want me.

MACLEOD. I wanted a wife, not a nymphomaniac.

MATA HARI. And you gave me sores. You gave your children sores. Syphilis is slurping up your brain even as we speak.

MACLEOD. You're what's eating my brain. Cannibal. Monstress. I should have gotten rid of you the minute I realized what you were.

MATA HARI. Then why didn't you?

MACLEOD. Because you're the mother of my children.

MATA HARI. Well, I'm the mother of somebody's children.

MACLEOD. What the hell is that supposed to mean?

MATA HARI. A man never really knows for sure, does he?

MACLEOD. I wonder how difficult it would be to kill you, if I just squeezed on your neck for a couple of hours.

MATA HARI. That would excite you, wouldn't it?

MACLEOD. It would be a tremendous relief, like having a boil lanced.

MATA HARI. And don't speak to me about my children. You stole my children from me.

MACLEOD. You forfeited all parental rights when you ran off to Paris to become a whore.

MATA HARI. I'm not a whore. I'm a dancer.

MACLEOD. You dance like a whore, you abandoned your daughter and you murdered my son.

MATA HARI. How can you say that to me? You know it's your fault our son died.

MACLEOD. My fault? Your neglect.

MATA HARI. He wasn't neglected. He was poisoned by the servant girl.

MACLEOD. I don't know what you're talking about.

MATA HARI. She poisoned him. You know she did.

MACLEOD. I know nothing of the kind. He ate some bad fish. She was a perfectly decent girl.

MATA HARI. She was your mistress. You snuck into her room every night for months to mount her like a goat. Do you think I didn't notice? It sounded like you were killing something in there.

MACLEOD. This is pure fantasy on your part.

MATA HARI. How can you look me in the face and lie to me like that?

MACLEOD. You're the pathological liar. Your entire life has been one ridiculous fabrication after another. Born in the jungles of Sumatra. Raised in a sacred Hindu temple on the banks of the Ganges. Tiger hunting with the Maharajah of Bangalore. What a lot of claptrap. You're a silly Dutch trollop. That's all you are. And to blame the death of my son on a poor, innocent servant girl –

MATA HARI. I blame YOU. You threw her away when you were done with her and she took up with one of your soldiers. You were jealous and had him whipped, so she poisoned your child.

MACLEOD. You're hallucinating.

MATA HARI. She confessed.

MACLEOD. She had a fever. She was delirious. And you are the most utterly shameless strumpet in the history of fornication. You have no right to judge me, let alone that poor unfortunate girl. It's shameful.

MATA HARI. I'm shameful? This from the man I once caught making his sister take off his underwear. Did you give her syphilis too? That might explain why she's always drooling.

MACLEOD. Let's just leave my sister's drooling out of this. You're not going to do yourself any good by blaming others for your own sins.

MATA HARI. Men are such hypocrites. When I was six, my father gave me a carriage pulled by goats. It's the last thing a man ever gave me without expecting me to sleep with him. When they want you, that's all they can see when they look at you, and it makes you hate them a little, hate the vile ones and have contempt for the weak ones. The men you can like you don't trust. The men you can trust bore you out of your mind. And yet most of the time I pity them. Their desire gives me power over them. And I like very much the feeling of having power. This is why I had to reinvent myself. All my life I let men tell me who I was and how I should behave, until I found myself alone and starving in Paris, and then I decided, that's it. No more of that. From this moment onwards, I will define myself. Mata Hari means sunrise, the edge of the day. And in that sunrise, your lost little wife died, and Mata Hari was born. So I suppose I have you to thank, for driving me out, and for carrying me off to the Indies in the first place.

MACLEOD. God, I wish I was there now.

MATA HARI. So do I. Anything would be better than this. Even life with you.

MACLEOD. You might be interested in knowing, just for the record, that I didn't actually put that advertisement in the paper myself. A friend put it in for a joke.

MATA HARI. A joke? I am not a joke. My life is not a joke.

MACLEOD. I thought you were, until I set eyes on you. From that moment I was a dead man.

(Pause.)

MATA HARI. I was not a very good wife. I didn't know what I was doing. Most of the time, when I behaved badly, I was just trying to get your attention. But you had no right to hit me.

MACLEOD. That point is arguable. But I suppose it wasn't entirely your fault. You really were a child.

(Pause.)

I sit under the sycamore trees by the canal, watching the women pass, and think about the Indies, and I can feel myself coming to attention. You had the look of a half-caste girl. Something exotic. I think that's what drew me to you. I always liked a half-caste girl. There is a kind of uncanny beauty that comes from the illicit mixing of bloods. Best of both worlds. Unexpected juxtaposition makes the heart pound. I dream about them still. But the climate's no good for a white man. Carry you home on a stretcher, or, more likely, in a box. Rots the body. Rots the mind. Rots the soul. Seventeen years of hacking through the jungle in the rain rots the soul.

MATA HARI. We did have some good times there, didn't we? Despite everything, there was some tenderness between us.

MACLEOD. And those damned giant rats. They made my flesh crawl. Eat the baby if you weren't careful. And you were never careful. That was not one of your specialties.

MATA HARI. Listen to me. If you still have even a drop of affection for me, please help me get out of this place. This is a horrible place. I'm dying here.

MACLEOD. You should have thought of that before you agreed to spy for the Germans.

MATA HARI. I didn't spy for the Germans. I spied for the French. At least, I tried to spy for the French. The Germans wanted me to spy for them. But I only pretended to spy for the Germans because that's what the French asked me to do. And then suddenly the French find my behavior suspicious because I'm doing exactly what they're paying me to do. Except they never paid me. I'll tell you how crazy these people are. The French sent me to Holland to spy on the Germans. But on the way, I was arrested in London by the English, who were convinced I was a mysterious woman named Benedix, who actually was a spy. When they finally realized I was not anybody named Benedix, they asked the French what to do with me, and the French told them not to let me go to Holland, where they themselves had sent me, because I was a German spy. So the English sent me to Spain, where the Dutch consul, who is a Frenchman, tried to recruit me to spy for Russia. What the hell is the matter with these people? Are all men insane? I admit that I have a restless soul. This is actually considered attractive in a man. Why is it so suspicious in a woman? That's probably why you all want to kill me. Because I can see through you. I can see what you are.

MACLEOD. You haven't the slightest idea what I am. You never did. I had to go out there every day, risking my life in the jungle. A woman couldn't possibly understand the sort of pressure a man is under, the kind of courage he needs –

MATA HARI. Courage. I have more courage than you do.

MACLEOD. That's absurd. I'm a soldier. Do you know how many people I've killed?

MATA HARI. You surrendered yourself to a system, a military structure that you let define you. I stood alone and defined myself. That takes courage.

MACLEOD. You danced around in various states of undress and told a goddamned pack of lies about yourself, that's what you did.

MATA HARI. They weren't lies. It was art. I was turning my own flesh and blood into a work of art. I created Mata Hari and then I became her. And people loved me. Everybody wanted to see me.

MACLEOD. They wanted to see you naked.

MATA HARI. I was rich. I was famous. I was the toast of Europe.

MACLEOD. And look where it's got you: a dank, filthy prison cell with your friends, the rats.

MATA HARI. Because they're afraid of me. They're afraid of me because they desire me. They believe I'm the person I pretend to be, only it scares the hell out of them, because they want me so much. That's the terrible thing about having created your own identity: you become trapped in it, and sometimes you long to return to being the nobody you were before you created it. But you can't get out.

MACLEOD. You made your bed. Now lay in it. You and your friends the rats.

MATA HARI. But I'm innocent.

MACLEOD. You took money from a German intelligence agent.

MATA HARI. I take money from everybody.

MACLEOD. This money was for spying on the French.

MATA HARI. But I didn't spy on the French.

MACLEOD. So your defense is that you're a liar and a thief?

MATA HARI. My defense is that I'm not a spy. I only took the money because the Germans never paid me for my last theatrical engagement in Berlin.

MACLEOD. Which Germans?

MATA HARI. Other Germans.

MACLEOD. Other Germans didn't pay you so you took money from these Germans?

MATA HARI. Exactly.

MACLEOD. That doesn't make any sense.

MATA HARI. Maybe not to you. Besides, I lost all my luggage in Switzerland.

MACLEOD. What the hell has your luggage got to do with it?

MATA HARI. I needed money to buy new luggage. How could I go to Holland with no luggage?

MACLEOD. So you went to Holland to spy for the Germans.

MATA HARI. I went to Holland to visit my lover in the Hague, Colonel Baron van der Capellen of the Second Regiment of Hussars. He's very rich. I knew I could get money from him. But not if I had no clothes. Well, of course, he liked me without my clothes, but in order to take your clothes off, you've got to have something to wear, and how could I bring anything to wear if I didn't have any luggage? Which is why I allowed myself to be accosted by a stranger while coming out of church in Amsterdam.

MACLEOD. Church? You go to church?

MATA HARI. I'm a very spiritual person. And it's a great place to meet rich, lonely old men. And this fellow turned out to be a banker named van der Schalk, who became my lover and was really very nice to me. I told him I was Russian, used the money he gave me to buy clothes, and then I left him and went back to the Baron.

MACLEOD. What's all that got to do with spying for the Germans?

MATA HARI. Absolutely nothing.

MACLEOD. Then why are you telling me this?

MATA HARI. To show you what I was actually doing when the French thought I was spying for the Germans.

MACLEOD. The Germans must have thought you were spying for them. Why else would they have paid you?

MATA HARI. How should I know what the Germans thought? If they thought I was working for them, it just proves what a good spy I was for the French. And if they didn't think I was working for them, what harm was done?

MACLEOD. If you're spying for the French, then why did they put you in prison?

MATA HARI. That's what I'd like to know. I come back with valuable information and they arrest me, throw me in this hell hole, refuse to let me talk to anybody, accuse me of all sorts of monstrous imaginary crimes, and bombard me with idiotic questions regarding things I know nothing about. What do they want from me? Why can't they just tell me what they want? I'm fluent in several languages and I don't understand men in any of them. And men have never understood me. Of course, nobody has ever understood me. Even when I was a child, I always felt like a creature from another planet. When my mother died I played the piano for hours, and people were scandalized, hearing me out the windows. They thought I was horribly callous. But that's how I felt. I needed to play the piano. Whose job is it to tell me how to grieve for my mother? Who can judge the depth of anybody else's grief? People have always projected their own desires and fears upon me. It's like I'm not actually anybody. I'm just who people think I am. Maybe I've always been a spy. Pretending I was somebody else. Invisible ink flows in my veins. My tears are made of it. You don't know me. I don't know you. Nobody knows anybody. It's all a shadow play. I have been celebrated all across the continent, and soon they'll all have forgotten I was ever here. And I've been locked up in this dark place so long I'm not sure what's real any more. I don't know if I'm dreaming or awake. I really think I might be losing my mind. It's all so absurd. One minute I'm certain they're going to realize it was all a terrible mistake and release me. And the next minute I'm terrified they're going to kill me. And the French don't tell you ahead of time when they're going to execute you. I think it's less trouble for them that way. They wake you up in the middle of the night, but they take care to make a lot of noise to let you know they're coming. Sometimes I dream that they're coming to kill me. But they won't. I can't believe they'd be so cruel. So stupid. Why can't they just admit that they're wrong? I cannot comprehend such massive, overwhelming stupidity and cowardice, even among men. If they shoot me, I don't want a blindfold. I want to look the bastards in the eye. I want them to remember me.

MACLEOD. Yes. That'll teach them a lesson.

MATA HARI. I've got to get out of here. If you can't help me yourself, can't you please just get word to my Russian lover, Vadime? They've been intercepting our letters. If he knew what was happening, he'd find a way to save me.

MACLEOD. He's blind.

MATA HARI. He isn't blind. Not entirely.

MACLEOD. Your Russian lover was blinded at the front. Ironic, isn't it, that all your life you've been manipulating men with your looks, and your one true love is blind.

MATA HARI. I don't care if he's blind. He'll help me somehow. He'll testify for me.

MACLEOD. He's already testified. He's sent them a letter stating that you were merely a prostitute he was acquainted with briefly and he wants nothing more to do with you. You can ask the French prosecutor if you like. So much for true love.

MATA HARI. Oh, God.

MACLEOD. God won't help you either.

MATA HARI. The one man on earth I thought I could trust, and he betrays me, too, just like all the rest.

MACLEOD. Love is made of betrayal. The end is always there in the beginning. We kill what we love, and what we love kills us. That's what love is. The most exquisite form of murder.

MATA HARI. He's exactly the same age our son would have been, if he'd lived.

(Pause.)

If you're not here to help me, then why did you come? Just so you could torture me?

MACLEOD. I didn't come to torture you. I came to bring you a present.

MATA HARI. A present?

MACLEOD. It's in the bag.

MATA HARI. You brought me a present?

MACLEOD. Go on. Look in the bag. It's not a snake. It won't bite you.

MATA HARI. What is it?

MACLEOD. Look in the bag and find out.

MATA HARI. *(Looking in the satchel.)* Nobody's brought me anything in so long. It's very thoughtful of you to –

(Pulling out a jeweled bra.)

It's my costume. Why have you brought my costume? What am I supposed to do with this?

MACLEOD. What you usually do with it. Dance for me.

MATA HARI. You want me to dance for you?

MACLEOD. You dance for everybody else. You've never danced for me.

MATA HARI. You might have come to see me dance at any time.

MACLEOD. Do you think I wanted to sit in the middle of a theatre full of men gaping at my wife while she took her clothes off? I told anybody who asked that I'd already seen you from every possible angle, and didn't need to see it again. But on those nights when I finally manage to get to sleep, I dream about the Indies, and I hear that music, and I see you dancing, in my dream. But I can't see you clearly. It's like you're behind some sort of gauze, like the shadow puppets in Java. Dance for me. If you want my help, that's the price. Dance. I want to see you dance. Just once before I die. Or before you die. Whichever comes first.

MATA HARI. You do love me after all.

MACLEOD. Rubbish.

MATA HARI. I knew it.

MACLEOD. You don't know anything. You're completely ignorant of yourself and everybody else. If you were a spy, you had to be the worst spy in the history of espionage.

MATA HARI. Bluster all you want. I know you're very angry at me. But deep in your soul, you have loved me all along. Thank you.

(She goes up to him, kisses him tenderly on the cheek.)

MACLEOD. It's nearly dawn. Do it now. And then perhaps I'll do something for you.

MATA HARI. All right. Why not?

(She disappears into the upstage shadows.)

MACLEOD. Where are you going?

MATA HARI. Back here, to change.

MACLEOD. You're shy? After having slept with a sizable percentage of the European population, and riding around naked on a white horse in front of a huge gathering of Lesbians, you're shy about changing clothes in front of your husband?

MATA HARI. *(From the darkness, off.)* I don't want to spoil the effect.

MACLEOD. The effect is that you prance around for a while pretending to dance while taking off your clothes. Hurry up. The sun's about to rise. It's nearly time.

MATA HARI. Time for what?

MACLEOD. We've got official business to transact here.

MATA HARI. What?

MACLEOD. *(Taking a piece of paper out of his pocket.)* Just attending to a couple of necessary formalities.

MATA HARI. Formalities?

MACLEOD. *(Peering at the paper.)* Forgot my damned spectacles.

MATA HARI. Your what?

MACLEOD. *(Finding his glasses.)* There they are. Lose my nose if it wasn't attached to my face.

(He puts on the glasses, scans the paper.)

Blah blah blah treason. Blah blah blah capital offense.

MATA HARI. What are you mumbling about?

MACLEOD. Blah blah firing squad. Here.

(Reading from the paper.)

In the name of the people of France –

MATA HARI. In the what?

MACLEOD. – the military government of Paris has rendered the following judgment –

MATA HARI. This is all so strange, you being here. I haven't been sleeping well, and being in prison plays tricks with your mind. It alters your sense of reality.

MACLEOD. You've always had an altered sense of reality. In fact, except perhaps in regards to sexual intercourse, you've never seemed to me to possess any discernible sense of reality whatsoever.

MATA HARI. All a person needs is a vivid imagination and a strong will.

MACLEOD. And the result is a dangerous lunatic.

MATA HARI. I had a strong suspicion that they've slipped something into my tea to make me sleep. That could be what's making everything seem so strange. I mean, you being here, even, is a little strange.

MACLEOD. Now I've lost my place. Where the devil was I?

MATA HARI. I mean, what's happened to the French?

MACLEOD. The most damned distracting woman in the history of nipples.

MATA HARI. It does rather have the feeling of a dream, doesn't it? Spying is like a dream. One creates an alternative reality. But I don't like betraying people.

MACLEOD. You've been betraying people all your life. Every breath you take is a betrayal. Your flesh is entirely made of betrayal.

MATA HARI. But it's not true. They mistook me for somebody else.

MACLEOD. Yes, well, so did I.

(Finding his place again.)

Here it is.

(Reading from the paper.)

– has rendered the following judgement: declaring that the woman Zelle, Marguerite Gertrude – called Mata Hari –

MATA HARI. Does it feel that way to you?

MACLEOD. – divorced wife –

MATA HARI. Like a dream?

MACLEOD. – divorced wife of one MacLood –

MATA HARI. The dance of Shiva is a kind of dream.

MACLEOD. Not MacLood, dammit. MacLeod. Stupid French. Tell them your own name and they'll correct you.

MATA HARI. Art is a kind of dream.

MACLEOD. – is guilty of espionage and intercourse with the enemy –

MATA HARI. Love is a dream.

MACLEOD. – well, intercourse is right –

MATA HARI. My whole life has been a kind of dream.

MACLEOD. – with the end of assisting his efforts.

MATA HARI. Like a giant puzzle, or a coded message.

MACLEOD. Therefore, in consequence –

MATA HARI. It's as if there are clues everywhere, if you can only recognize them.

MACLEOD. Will you shut up and let me do this?

MATA HARI. I mean that what appears to be reality is actually written in some sort of code.

MACLEOD. What the hell are you blathering about?

MATA HARI. One needs to be one of God's spies, to break the code.

MACLEOD. In consequence –

MATA HARI. There are spies everywhere. Everything is made of espionage.

MACLEOD. – the aforementioned council –

MATA HARI. Everything's actually something else. Everybody is actually somebody else.

MACLEOD. – condemns her to pain of death.

MATA HARI. *(Appearing, in costume.)* There. It still fits. It's been so long since I've worn it. How do I look?

(Brief pause while he stares at her.)

I said, how do I look?

MACLEOD. *(Rather hypnotized in spite of himself.)* Quite astonishingly beautiful, actually.

MATA HARI. It's a wonder, if I do. They won't let me take baths here. There've been times when I'd have sold my soul for a bar of soap and a telephone. I've always been a clean person. What are you looking at?

MACLEOD. I just – I'd forgotten how beautiful you are.

MATA HARI. What were you going on about while I was changing?

MACLEOD. Nothing of any consequence. Just talking to myself.

MATA HARI. You need to be careful of that. I was doing that a lot when I first got here, but now I prefer talking to the rats. They really are very good listeners. Better than most men. All right. I'm afraid you must imagine the music.

(We hear the sound of the gamelan music playing softly.)

And also, there before me, the idol of Shiva, the god of destruction and transformation, for whom I dance.

MACLEOD. Yes. Whatever. Just get on with it.

MATA HARI. *(Striking a pose, holding it a moment, and then beginning to dance.)* My dance is a dance of worship, and also a plea for justice.

MACLEOD. Justice?

MATA HARI. And for vengeance.

MACLEOD. Yes. Vengeance.

(MATA HARI dances. MACLEOD watches, stone faced, but fascinated.)

MATA HARI. The dance is a sacred poem. Each gesture is a word. Each word is music. I begin my dance covered in veils. I appeal to the god Shiva for vengeance against those who have done evil towards me. I peel off the veils, one by one, signifying illusions cast off, levels of understanding reached, spiritual growth.

(She drops the first veil.)

MACLEOD. It's all rubbish, of course. And yet there is a certain demented beauty about this. Uncanny. Not quite human.

MATA HARI. Some elements of oriental dance are derived from marionettes.

MACLEOD. You know nothing about oriental dance. You never studied anything. You've never been to India. Your biography is a pack of ridiculous lies. And yet –

MATA HARI. Brahma, Vishnu, and Shiva. Creation, life and destruction. You must imagine that I dance with the blade of the knife in my teeth. A sword in my fist. The purple belt unrolls. It is the flow of blood.

(She drops the second veil.)

MACLEOD. What blood is that? Whose blood?

MATA HARI. The blood that spurts out when I plunge the knife into the heart of my unfaithful lover.

(She drops the third veil.)

MACLEOD. *(Staring at her as she dances.)* Unfaithful. Yes. Vengeance. Marionettes. The white mist gathers over the river. Scorpions under the flower pots. A carriage pulled by goats. The screaming of the monkeys in my dreams.

MATA HARI. The temple where I dance may be depicted elaborately or simply. It doesn't matter.

MACLEOD. Desire is a kind of fever dream. A naked half caste girl. So beautiful.

MATA HARI. We move from destruction through incarnation into creation. That is what I am dancing. From despair and humiliation, along the Pathway of Rapture to the Gate of Ecstasy.

(She drops the fourth veil.)

MACLEOD. But treacherous. It is all a lie. All made of betrayal. She is not what she seems.

MATA HARI. I am the temple.

(She drops the fifth veil.)

MACLEOD. One must not allow one's self to be seduced. She is all made of treason.

MATA HARI. I am the sacred text. I am the dance.

MACLEOD. It's dawn. The sun is rising. Time now.

MATA HARI. And at the conclusion of the dance –

(She drops the sixth veil.)

MACLEOD. Ready.

MATA HARI. At that moment, just before the dropping of the final veil –

MACLEOD. Aim.

MATA HARI. I offer myself up as a sacrifice to the god, and all is revealed.

(She is about to drop the last veil.)

MACLEOD. Fire.

(Sound of the firing squad, very loud. **MATA HARI** *falls, shot many times. The music stops. Silence.*

Just a few faint jungle sounds. **MACLEOD** *walks over to the body, takes out his revolver.*

And one final act of love: a clean shot to the head.

(He points the revolver down at her head. Blackout as we hear the sound of the shot.)

NOTEBOOK: MATA HARI

It's the night before her execution. She's alone in her rat-infested cell. She has been in prison for months, and her mental condition is confused at best. Her drunken, abusive husband MacLeod appears to her. She dreams or hallucinates a last performance. Seven veils.

There is no credible evidence that she spied for the Germans, but the French authorities are determined to execute her. That male establishment which has ruined her life, which she briefly felt she had power over, has joined forces to kill her.

MacLeod represents in her mind all the men who have used, abused and betrayed her. She has triumphed over them for a while, but in the end they will destroy her. When informed of her execution, MacLeod reportedly said, "Whatever she has done in her life, she did not deserve that." But in her mind, he is the embodiment of all the men who have failed her and are now destroying her.

It would seem to have been her promiscuity that made them think she would be a good spy, and then, later, that she must be a spy for the enemy. Somehow, a woman who slept with that many men must be guilty. The sum of our desire is also the sum of our fears.

When she saw how many persons had lined up outside the prison to see her taken to her execution, she commented dryly: "All these people. What a success."

Four days after her execution, her one time handler in French intelligence and later her chief accuser, Georges Ladoux, was arrested as a German spy himself. He was later released, but if he was not a German spy, it's difficult to explain his bizarre behavior towards Mata Hari, who he encouraged to spy for the French and then brutally hung out to dry with a mixture of lies and half-truths.

I was looking into the night, and saw only night. After years of groping in the dark, we stand on the edge of utter strangeness. Ahead of us, a horrific, vertiginous descent.

The gamelan is a traditional ensemble of musical instruments popular in Java and Bali, tuned together and designed to be played together. There are xylophone and metallophone components, along with gongs, drums, flutes, and plucked strings. From the Javanese word for hammer, which is used strike the various metal tubes and gongs. This music is smooth, elegant, and intricate.

All of these things, said Machen, are dreams and shadows which hide the real world from our eyes. There is a real world, beyond this glamour and this vision, as beyond a veil.

It is the lifting of successive veils that forms the basic structure of Mata Hari's dance. Each time a veil drops to the floor, one sees a bit more clearly the mystery which is incarnate in Mata Hari's body. When the final veil drops, what is revealed is not just her flesh, but the place from which we have come. Her body is a powerful symbol, a portal through which we reconnect to a distant memory of having once emerged, bloody and screaming, into the harsh light, and to which we spend our lives longing desperately to return. We want to be inside the goddess again. This is the hidden significance of intercourse: not to perpetuate the race, but to somehow return to the darkness inside her.

To lift the veil, says Machen, is to seek the Great God Pan, ancient god of the woods, ancestor of the horned devil. The eerie sense, when alone in the woods, of the presence of some ancient other, predator or god, in which state the hackles rise on the back of the neck, is much akin to what we feel when we experience a powerful work of art, or see a woman naked. It is the true holiness, the uncanny sense of union with ultimate mysteries. For all the sideshow hokum surrounding it, this is what Mata Hari's dance was intended to put one in touch with: that eerie, mystical sense of union with the utter strangeness of the other.

But in her dream, or what flashes through her brain as she is being executed, she is killed before the final veil is dropped. They kill her in part because they don't want to confront the answer to the mystery of their existence. Terrified of ultimate revelations, we murder those who would supply them. In the end, we are too terrified to know.

How much she actually took off in performance varied. In the oriental dances that made her famous, she seems to have left on a jeweled bra, perhaps because she felt that her breasts were not her best feature, and perhaps another strategically placed jeweled ornament at her genitals. She was probably never the same twice. Like an accident or a crime, each witness told a different story. She was the embodiment of what each onlooker desired and feared.

Here on the shore of the Baltic I walk in the cold winter air. Different aspects of my soul are in various stages of completion. All knowledge comes to us in fragments, but in each fragment all the other fragments are reflected.

She once rode a horse into her lover's mansion, up and down the main staircase, side saddle.

The veil is the theatre. It is the play of Shiva, the cosmic dancer, lord of destruction, passionate lover, loyal partner, cousin of Dionysus. To worship Shiva is not to adore names and forms but the onrushing torrent of change which continually creates and destroys individual existences. It is the waterfall, we are the drops, the foam. The dancer becomes united with the force that has created and will destroy her. Sorrow and joy are transcended in the ecstasy of the dance. The difference between us and God is that God knows he's wearing a mask. When he takes off the mask, nothing is there. We are the trees, God is the forest.

Each play you are working on becomes the mirror into which one gazes. Each person you love is a holy text you study as if it were the only book in existence. To love any creature is to study the deepest mysteries of the universe. In each drop is reflected the whole. God is an infinity of reflections.

Someone is following me.
Of course someone is following you. Women who look like you are always followed.
No, but this is something else. Two men.
I'm sure you can handle it.

How does a spy express her love?
invisible ink.

Hoogslag and Sneck
fell on my neck.

There are scorpions under the flower pots.

Why does he ask her to dance? Does he really want to see it, or is it simply a device to distract her from the immanence of her execution? He wants to see it, is horrified and disgusted by it, is nevertheless spellbound, aroused and in despair.

One witness to Mata Hari's performance said that he felt "an emotion which defies analysis and leaves one with the impression of a dream."

Vadime has lost his sight in the war. How ironic that it took a blind man to love me. The dark red secrets of the mystery of the body.

I do not wish to be an ornament, or a curiosity.
Then why have you gone to so much damned trouble to make yourself into one?

When she was invited to dance in *The King of Lahore* for the Monte Carlo ballet, the prima ballerina there, La Zambelli, is said to have remarked, "She is as much an Indian dancer as I am a Chinese waiter."

She wanted desperately to play the dancer Salome in Strauss's opera based on the Oscar Wilde play, but her efforts to persuade anyone else that she could do it were unsuccessful. "I am the only person who can dance the mind of Salome," she said.

Later she was painted naked as Salome, fondling the head of John the Baptist. After her execution, her own head was removed.

She died bravely, refusing a blindfold, looking her assassins in the eye.

Full moon. Shedding of blood.
A lotus woman cannot be permitted.
Eyes of the fawn.

The train leaves
but she remains
on the platform
in a kind of trance.

When there is something
I don't understand
I will knock at any door.
But often nobody is home.

What information do you have
about the submarine?
It sinks.
I know it sinks. But does it rise?

Not often.

Have you been to Antwerp?
Have you frolicked in Brussels?

I have dropped the sugar bowl
on the linoleum.
It was the bluejays.
They startled me.
They know something.
They are God's spies.

POEM FOR MATA HARI

Down a long, dark passage
the recurring hallucination
that I am trapped in someone else's dream,
wild panic of the imagination:
a diabolical visitation
in a padded cell

(unscrew the mirrors from the walls)

studying to discover at what hour
a woman is most likely to allow

something is hidden in the words:

(take the key out of your pocket)

(put the kettle on
and unbutton your dress)

(she bathes in warm milk)

Having mounted her in the tall grass

(the executioner fears the clown)

she is an orchid among dandelions
a raspberry among wild boars

(I'll carve her into gobbets)

drag the body to the pit
scattering pieces along the way
to lighten one's burden

(you discredit our mystery)

then dive into the burning lake below

Marina

For Tatyana Kot

MARINA was first presented along with *Mata Hari* on June 15, 2013 at the Robert Moss Theatre, 440 Lafayette Street, New York City, by Nylon Fusion Theatre Company as part of the Planet Connections Theatre Festivity, with:

MARINA. . . . . Tatyana Kot

Directed by Ivette Dumeng.

The rest of the creative team was:

Scenic Designer	Tijana Bjelajac
Sound Designer	Andy Evan Cohen
Costume Designer	Hope Governali
Lighting Designer	Dan Stearns
Choreography	Natasa Trifan
Stage Manager	Laura Malseed
Publicist	Bunch of People
Assistant Stage Manager	Kimberly Flores
Graphic Design and Property Master	Greg Kanyicska
Doll Designer	Juliana Francis Kelly
House Manager	Juan Garcia
Cover Photography	Graeme Malcolm (Mata Hari), Theik Smith (Marina)

CHARACTER

MARINA TSVETAYEVA – a Russian poet, in her forties.

SETTING & TIME

Elabuga, a town in Russia, on August 31, 1941.

The set could be a room with a red lantern, a blue wooden rocking chair on which sits a little girl doll, a wooden table with wooden chair, on the table an old pack of tarot cards, and a coiled up length of rope on an old trunk. But perhaps there is no set at all, and it's just Marina, in a circle of light on a bare stage.

The music is two Etudes by Scriabin, Opus 8: Number 11, in B flat minor, and Number 12, in D sharp minor.

*(In the darkness, we have been listening to Scriabin's Etude Number 12, Opus 8. Lights up on **MARINA**, a woman in her forties, in August of 1941. When the music ends, she speaks.)*

MARINA. On the street of the Three Ponds
there was a child who stole apricots.
Welcome to the Gingerbread House, they said.
This is not the chapel of unexpected joy.
The birds have eaten all your bread crumbs.
The wallpaper hangs in tatters.
There's a nail driven into the crossbeam
where the horses are tied up.
And here is a strong piece of rope.
I have appointments to keep in the past.

But there are blank spaces in my head.
Why can't I remember your face?
All I can see is a white blur like a flour sack.
Ghosts covered in slowly falling snow.
Those who are pitied. Those who are kissed.
There is no wall between the living and the dead,
between what was and what is.
The past is happening all around us,
the dead are all around us.
We live here with ghosts.
The ghosts are more real than we are.

And the French police keep asking me
absurd questions I don't understand.
Poisoned chocolates? I don't
know anything about
poisoned chocolates.

I walk into the empty church at night.
The congregation is silent.
There is a painting with

little black trees like sticks.

Pushkin has been shot.
They help him to the sleigh.
Soon he will die.
The wind billows the curtains

as if they were with child.
On the opposite wall is a portrait
of a dead woman. Somebody's mother.
Not mine. I am the child
of the second wife.
She plays the piano in another room.

> *(Sound of Scriabin's Etude #11 in B flat minor, Opus 8, being played very softly on a piano through what follows.)*

My father can't forget his first wife.
Her children can't forgive him
for marrying my mother.
My mother can't forget
the man who took her innocence.
It's horrible what love does to you, she said.
Play the piano instead.

Then someone grabs my shoulder.
It's my dead godmother.
Beware of your mother, she says.
And I realize I'm
about to be devoured.

My mother thought I hated music.
But I just hated practicing.
I couldn't stand being forced
to play what other people

wanted me to play –
the idiotic little exercises
invented by some ridiculous mediocrity
who could read music perfectly
but who played like a corpse.
How could any good thing possibly come
from something so mechanical and stupid?
I wanted to feel, when I played,
like I felt when I listened to
Tschaikovsky or Scriabin.

And this torture went on forever
because for a child there is no future.
There is only an eternal present.
Trying to force beauty –
this is how love is killed.

My sister was lucky:
she played horribly.
Mostly the wrong notes,
but, mercifully, not very loud.
My curse was that I was just good enough
to give my mother hope.
But at the piano, as in life,
I can never follow the score.
I always play better by heart.

God doesn't like this. God lives in the piano.
I polish his hard black skin until
I can see a strange girl's face reflected in him.

As a child I knew an old man who
whispered to me his tragic secret: God
beat his brother to death with a cucumber, and
his punishment was that his penis fell off.

On the other side of the door,
something is waiting for me.
I sensed it that night in the orchard.

Someone standing in the garden
among the apple trees,
drawn by my green eyes.

There was a time when I
was the goddess in the bushes.
My tutor was in love with me
and the friend he sent to propose to me
was in love with me
but also with my sister.
In those days love was all made of
triangles and quadrangles.
We believe these youthful passions
are everything and then
we decide they are nothing
and when they're gone forever
we want them back so desperately.

I'd write poems about these loves
and then my mother would burn them.
Why does a mother burn her daughter's poems?
Because she knows instinctively
that words can kill.
But my life is a rough draft.
To understand even the simplest thing
I must first turn it into poetry.

I stopped playing the piano
when she died.

> *(A pause in the music which corresponds to that distinctive measure of silence just before the end of the Scriabin etude. Then it resumes.)*

But now the music
has got into my poems.
The soul absorbs all things
and turns them into art.

She couldn't understand that what I wanted

was to descend into the dark lagoon of the
piano and be completely enveloped by it.
Drown in it.

(The music stops.)

And yet I have always feared the sea.
The sea is too much like love.
It swallows you like
a crocodile swallows a duck.
That's not the sea, I said,
when I first saw it.
That can't be the sea.
That's not at all like the sea.
What have they done with the sea?
The sea is something else entirely.
I've always been after something else.
What we can speak of is always less
than what is actually the case
but the love in your head is always more real
than the object of love itself.

A gentle boy with enormous eyes,
collecting small stones on the shore.
If he picks that one up,
I will marry him.
You and I will get married some day
when we are all drowned.

In all my sleepless nights
I am in love with you.
In all my sleepless nights
I listen for you.
While gravediggers stir
in the morning.

Are you dead now?
Yes. I think you are dead.
And all the while I never knew you.

Are you sorry that you've loved me?

Marriage is, on the whole,
a good thing, because anything
that's being hurt regains its innocence.
But it's a sin to think you ever
really know another person.
The heart of another
is a dark forest.
And all the while,
when I was busy feeding
rabbits in my dreams,
you were giving people
poisoned chocolates.

When you go to the fair, Mother, I said,
bring me back the Devil in a bottle.
But you must never become attached
to a thing that can break.

I lay out the cards again and again.
The game is not what we think we're playing.
We are not playing cards.
The cards are playing us.
The Devil lives in the cards.

The Devil bites deep, like a tick.
The Devil sleeps on my chest.
When I squeeze the lower part of his tube
he jumps. What a wicked girl,
to make the Devil jump.

The first mark of the Devil's chosen
is complete disconnection
from everyone and everything. Exile.
Peer into the looking glass and
invite him into your soul if you dare.
But under the green Venetian mirror,
in the labyrinth of mirrors reflecting mirrors,

the only currency is death.

Something is lurking in this place,
a strange animal who whispers
to me from another room.
I go up the staircase, hesitate, then enter.
If I stare into the darkness
I can just make him out.

The Devil is sitting on my sister's bed.
Naked, in gray skin, like a Great Dane,
with whitish-blue eyes. Smooth,
clean-shaven, body of a lioness,
small horns like ears,
and a long tail.
I recognize him by his eyes:
Cold. Clear. Deadly.
He sits. I stand. And I love him.

I have not mastered the game of being loved.
When I love something, I consume it.
It turns to something inside me
which is fatal to happiness,
mine and the beloved's.
Poets have a genius for
loving unsuitable objects.
My way of loving
is to say goodbye.

I think only those who skim on the surface
like mayflies can be happy.
I was not made for this existence.
I need every day to be madness.
Everything must be a catastrophe.
I can't stand causing pain
and I can't help causing it.
I can love dozens of people
but when anybody rejects me

I feel as if I was skinned alive.
But I must be in love.
I must always be plunging headlong
into a vortex of passion.
The object of the passion
is not so important
as the passion itself.
The object is misunderstood
and mostly invented.
When the object retreats
or proves unworthy
I fall into the abyss of despair
which makes me receptive
to a new object.
It's the fatal rhythm
of passion and despair that matters.
Ecstasy, despair, and ecstasy again.
This is the rhythm of sex and art.

All love is self delusion.
Truth is a traitor.
Love chills you to the bone,
burns to white heat, then kills.
The river of love needs flesh
and flows through Hell.
We all end up in Hell.
Every gift of God exists
so it can be ruined.
In the end we have nothing to protect us.
In the end, we have nothing.

I loved my first two children very much,
but I didn't think about them every second.
How boring that would be. That is not love,
I told myself. That is a sickness. And yet
I have been very ill.

Ariadne brings me a drawing.
Look, Mommy, she says. Look what I've drawn.
What is this? I say. Is this supposed to be
a person? I don't see what sort of person
it could be. It's got a head like a cabbage.
And there's a different number of fingers
on each hand, and both are the wrong number.
Has this person been in some sort of an
accident with a threshing machine?
And look at those skinny arms and legs.
Who do we know who has seven fingers,
arms and legs like matchsticks
and a cabbage for a head?

All right. You think I'm horrible.
But I'm her mother.
It's my job to be horrible.
If I don't tell her the truth, who will?
Should we praise our children for not paying attention?
Drawing badly, like writing badly or loving badly
is not having the courage to pay attention.
I'm not going to encourage
sloppy looking at the world.
That sort of thing can get a person killed.
A child has got to learn to see things,
not just look at them.

And no, you can't play the piano.
You must be a poet.
I won't have any child of mine
playing a damned piano.
As I hear myself say this,
hundreds of reflections of my mother
are smiling sadly back at me
in a house of mirrors.

Also, the child laughs at clowns.
Shame on you.
I am very disappointed in you.
We must never laugh at persons
with big feet and red noses,
who are always falling on bananas.
We should pity such people.
Don't look at the clowns.
Look at the animals.
It's by looking at animals
that we see our true humanity.
All that we learn from clowns
is that everybody here is clowns.
It is all one big clown show.

Except for your father, of course.
Not that I can say I knew him.
I was married to him for many years
but that is a different thing.
Rue is for repentance.
but there's none of that in my basket.
And yet, how could he do that?
How could he murder people
and not tell me?

I never knew my husband.
I never knew any man.
I never knew myself.
Writing I knew. Writing
is like dreaming. Writing
is not something you do.
Writing is something that
happens to you, like love.

But where does this tenderness come from?
We can only pray that love without fiction
is not itself a fiction. They tell me I have spent

my life imagining those I love.
First, that is a lie. And second,
what is not imagination?
We can't touch reality directly.
Everything we know is in our head.
All love is in the head.

For five years, during war and revolution,
I thought my husband was dead. So who could
blame me for sleeping with poets and actors?
Of course, I was unfaithful before that,
and after, but still, one must be in love
to write poetry, and being in love with
a new person is so much more inspiring
than being in love with the same old person.

Mandelstam, for example, had eyes
like a camel. I liked the way he kissed
my elbows. Only a very great poet
could become so deeply aroused
by a woman's elbows.
And Pasternak, so wise in his writing,
in his life, not so much.
He wanted me but not, in the end,
enough to do much about it.

Men find so many different ways
to be unsatisfactory,
especially poets, and I'm always
looking for one to worship.
When I offered myself to Rilke
he was so horrified
he dropped dead on the spot.

They love you, and then they don't.
It's as simple as that.
And if they are permitted to be

ruthless about their happiness,
then so must you be.
Otherwise, love makes you
a perpetual victim.
And a goddess is not a victim.
Others sacrifice to the goddess.
Unless the goddess chooses
to fling herself
into the abyss.

And I never stopped loving my husband.
I just loved other people, too.
Why does everybody always want
to put me in a box? Let me alone.
I'm restless by nature. I like to walk
the streets at night. I love deeply,
but can't be loyal for long. I know
it hurts him, but it's not my fault.
I love him, and he knows it.
Isn't that enough?

And if I sleep with a woman now and then
it's only because women are better lovers.
I'm sorry, but men don't understand
the slightest thing about a woman's body.
You can love them, you can enjoy them,
up to a point, but how can a man
really make you happy?
A woman knows what to do.

I can never completely possess a man
because something's always missing in them.
All men are fragments of something else.
Only women are complete. And then
only sometimes. We have the capacity
to contain things. Men can only poke around
in the dark. I'm not being unfaithful.

I'm just being honest. I need
to exhale myself into another,
and breathe the other into me.
A poet must feed her soul or it dies.

The only thing that matters
is absolute surrender.
Nothing else is real.

To love is to cherish a monomania,
a territory strange and unexplored.
But it's much easier to love than to be loved.
To love makes you alive, but to be loved
is exhausting, and makes me uneasy.
I should give up loving people.
Just animals and trees.
Love is what kills you.

The man I really love is Pushkin.
I've been in love with Pushkin
since I was a little girl.
It's an old story, really.
Girl loves poet. Poet is dead.
Well, it's not my fault he's dead.
I didn't kill him.

Why do I love the dead more than the living?
Why do I love the wolf more than the lamb?

Pushkin infected me with love
and nobody else quite measures up.
But I keep looking.
In one lover after another.
And who has the right to judge me?
Whose business is it
who I love or don't love?
God is not sitting in Heaven
counting my lovers.
He's got better things to do.

He's got babies to kill.

If you haven't struggled to feed your children
with no money in a cold city in time of war,
don't presume to judge me for reaching out
for a little happiness, a little comfort.
In our flat in Moscow during the war
we burned the furniture to keep warm.
The only meat we had was horse meat.
People were eating dogs and corpses.

And at the age of two years and ten months
my daughter Irina died of starvation
in the orphanage where my friends
convinced me to put her so
she wouldn't die of starvation.

A sweet little creature
who spent all her time
rocking back and forth
and singing.

When I had to go out,
I tied her to a blue chair
so she wouldn't hurt herself.
When I close my eyes I see her.
Rocking back and forth
in that blue chair, singing.

You give your love to any mortal creature
and all you're left with, in the end,
is a little pile of bones.
Never become attached
to a thing that can break.

Then, after the war, and the revolution,
to be in exile. Of course, all poets are
in exile. We are never really home.
But to be away from Russia is
to be in exile from one's language,

to be speaking when nobody
can understand, which is bad enough
for a sane person, but for a writer
is death.

In Czechoslovakia we lived
in villages with names like
Horni Mokropsy – Upper Wet Dogs –
and Dolni Mokropsy – Lower Wet Dogs.
A barking dog on a chain.
An outhouse in the back.
And yet I was almost happy there.
I was able to write. I wrote.

But then we moved to Paris.
Everybody's always going on
about how wonderful Paris is,
especially the French, who are greatly
enamored of themselves, and the
Americans, who are mentally deficient,
and I must admit it's a rather pretty doll house,
and I was fussed over there until
I insulted the critics and managed
to offend everyone by committing
the crime of telling the truth.
And there was freedom, of a sort.
But what good is freedom if
nobody speaks your language?

In Russia, if they don't like what you write,
they kill you. It's an honest reaction, at least.
In Paris I can write what I please
but who's going to read it?
All the Russians there are dead.
Take a Russian out of Russia
and what have you got?
A dead Russian.

All Russians in exile
are dead souls.

Actually, that's not true. I hear
these things coming out of my mouth,
and ask, who said that? And why?
Because nothing is real till you say it.
Before then, it's just something
you hear in your head, like a dream.
Words are the most powerful form of magic.
In Paris I might as well
be speaking in tongues.
I am a soul unacquainted with limits
surrounded by imbeciles.
And under the best circumstances
I am intelligible only in terms
of paradox, of contradictions,
of the simultaneous existence
of all times and places. So what
difference does it make what language
I'm misunderstood in?

And as I am misunderstood,
so I misunderstand.
Never presume to know the last
word about any other soul.
The heart of another
is a dark forest.

My husband I thought I knew so well
he bored me even as I loved him,
until one day the French police
haul me in, and ask me a lot
of bewildering questions,
blathering on about espionage
and poisoned chocolates
and telling me my husband is a spy,

my husband's an assassin.
My gentle, innocent,
helpless husband, who
plays in the water with the children
like a little boy.

It's all so ridiculous.
I can't make any sense of it.
Reality should not be
so much like the circus.
A hall of mirrors,
with animals and clowns.
Why can't it be a poem?

I'm so confused by their questions
I start lecturing them about
Racine and Moliere,
people the French police
have apparently never heard of,
so they decide I must be feeble minded
and let me go. And then when I get home,
I find out that my husband
has fled to Moscow.

I don't hear from him for weeks.
I'm absolutely frantic.
And when I finally get a letter from him,
what does he say to me?
Does he proclaim his innocence?
Does he explain about the poisoned chocolates?
Does he tell me how much he misses me?
Does he tell me he wants to make
passionate love to me?
No. He says he misses the French movies.

French movies? He misses the French movies?
Is there anything in the world
more stupid than French movies?

And so, deciding this must be
a secret code, I start
going to the movies, where I hope
to find some sort of clue
as to what the hell is going on.
But all I find is phantoms
gliding back and forth
in the darkness.

And nobody would speak to me now.
They can't believe I didn't know
my husband was a murderer.
And my daughter and my sister
and my husband, all in Russia,
kept begging me to join them.
And my son kept nagging at me to go back.
I suppose I thought if I took him there,
where the boy imagined he wanted to be,
then he'd love me.

All of my instincts told me not to do it.
But having already murdered one child
and neglected another,
I couldn't bear to lose this last one, too.
Love makes us stupid.
Love is what kills us, in the end.

So we go back to Russia and soon
they've arrested my sister.
They've arrested my daughter.
They've arrested my husband.
They've arrested all my friends,
most of the poets, and nearly
everybody with a brain.
And now I'm stuck here with my son,
upon whom I have showered so much affection
that he of course has absolute contempt for me,

for bringing him to such a dismal place.

There is only emptiness here.
Eight million in concentration camps,
and God knows how many murdered.
And all for politics.
What do I care about politics?
Politics is a self-evident abomination
from which nothing but further
abominations can be expected.
No matter what system I live under,
I must write like a wolf howls, or die.
But if I write from my soul here,
they will kill me.

So I survive by translating
the work of others, like a vampire.
Translation isn't writing. Not for me.
It's more like cannibalism.
How can a person like me
live without writing?

They want me to write for the Party.
To write for the sake of politics
is like being a whore without the sex.
I don't know where writing comes from.
But I know if one writes to please somebody else
the soul dies, and then the writer dies.

There are many souls in me,
waiting to get out.
Creation is like dreaming.
One writes in delirium.
One is pulled along by wild horses
with no idea where one's going.
One must write as if God was watching you
but tell the truth anyway.
And this is why they fear and hate me.

If I betray the voices,
what have I got left?
If I betray the voices
I am nothing.

I am called brave for
refusing to cooperate. The truth is,
I'm afraid of everything.
Eyes. Night. Footsteps
behind me in the darkness.
Wolf? Panther? Lynx?
I'm so nearsighted,
it could be anything.
But most of all, I fear myself.
I fear not writing honestly.
Here in the madhouse
of the inhuman, all
a sane person can do
is refuse.

I want to go to sleep, but now I can't.
And if I do, who knows
if I'll wake up again?
And if so, to what?
To Stalin's world.
A man so paranoid
he trusts no one but Hitler,
his fellow homicidal maniac,
who generously repays his trust
by invading Russia –
the stupidest move the history
of Western civilization.
Ask Napoleon.

They are fire-bombing Moscow.
They've got my clumsy son
diffusing unexploded bombs.

I had to get him out of there.
They're shipping writers to the country.
They think we'll be less dangerous
among the cows.
So we got on the train
and ended up here
in a place God has forgotten.
No money. No work. No food. No hope.
Just a nail in the crossbeam
where they once tied horses,
and a coil of rope.

I have failed at life.
I have written suicide notes
for everyone but myself.
My only salvation
has been the word.
And now even that is gone.

Of course, whatever you want,
you're given the opposite.
The trick is to take what you're given
and make something of it. I know that.
If you're afraid of wolves,
stay out of the woods.
But now I'm so lost in the forest
I will never find my way back.
The birds have eaten my bread crumbs.
I have come to the Gingerbread House,
and they're heating up the oven.

What do they think I've been doing?
Do they think I've been playing some stupid game?
This is the structure of my soul
I am ripping out of my flesh
and turning into words.
Do you find me too romantic?

Too passionate? Too violent?
I don't give a damn what you think.
I am not here to make pretty rhymes
about tractors for the Party.
I can't help it if I don't belong here.
I'm a poet. I don't belong anywhere.

Geese flying over.
Tea from elderberry branches.
Those who can't sleep
will soon sleep forever.
Somewhere tonight
somebody is drowning.
I think it's me.
I don't want to die.
I just want not to exist.
At least not like this.

A stone is cast in a pond.
The sky as red as a lake of blood.
There is so much mist here
you walk around
surrounded by the dead.
As one grows older, gradually
one loses one's sense of reality.
What is this strangeness?
Who are these walking ghosts?
To take into your phantom hand
the phantom hand of another –

When he smells love, Death comes running
like the gardener when somebody's
stealing from his orchard.
Love is the sin that
cannot go unpunished.

If my husband is dead,
then I am the one responsible.
This bizarre impersonation of a spy,

arranging murders for a psychopath.
Was it all to get my attention?
To show me he wasn't the person
I took for granted? He gave some poor man
a box of poisoned chocolates
and his reward is that
now they have killed him.

Look how his wings are broken.
They mistook him for something human,
and now he is dead forever.

I turn up the last card.
I know what it will be:
the hanged man.
Take the nail they use
to tether the horses.
Tie a rope to it.
Somebody has set fire
to the past.

Did I win, or lose?
Why must it be a game?
Love comes in poisoned chocolates.

I close my eyes and find myself.
moving across the waters
to the shore of the Red Room
where Pushkin waits in the closet.
Red girl in the red strawberry flood,
under a blood red moon,
trapped in a red bottle.

A woman who is starving
gives up her daughter to an orphanage
so she'll have something to eat,
and the child starves to death there.
What can you make of that?
You can make a poem.

But what good will that do her?
It will do you a little good, perhaps,
but not enough to save you.
Or anybody else.

If you listen, you can hear
somebody playing the piano
in another room.

>*(Sound of the Scriabin Etude #11 played softly.)*

I went to visit the house
where I was a child,
on the Street of the Three Ponds
where I stole the apricots.
They had taken the place apart
for firewood, piece by piece.
There was nothing left
but desolation.
The house is gone
but the Devil is still sitting there
in the middle of the ruins,
waiting for me.

I'll tell you the secret of the Red Room,
what Pushkin revealed to me
before he kissed my lips and died:

God is the Devil, he said.
God is the Devil,
the Devil is God,
and the murdered thing is love.
The murdered thing is always love.

I have been translated out
of the original tongues,
and now there are no more words.
Only a hook, and a coil of rope.

In my dream,

my mother plays the piano
in an empty house.

From this point on,
your life begins.

> *(The light fades on her and goes out. In the darkness, the music ends.)*

NOTEBOOK: MARINA

It is August, 1941. The poet Marina Tsvetayeva is deciding whether or not to take her life. These are her thoughts just before she makes her decision. Live or die? Which is best? She has neglected her husband and lost her children because of her obsession with writing, which has often been fueled by her passionate relationships with others. Now she realizes she never knew him to begin with, and does not know her children, either. Writing has been all she has, and when it is no longer possible, there seems to be no other course of action.

A brief chronology of the poet's life

1892 Born in Moscow.

1902-4 Mother ill. Family travels to Italy, Switzerland, Germany.

1905 Yalta, Crimea.

1906 Mother dies. Family back to Moscow.

1909 Studies French literature in Paris. First affair.

1910 Dresden. Moscow. *Evening Album* published.

1912 Marries Sergei Efron. *The Magic Lantern* published. Italy, France, Germany. Birth of daughter Ariadna.

1913 *From Two Books* published. Father dies.

1914 Affair with Sofia Parnok.

1916 St Petersburg. Affair with Osip Mandelstam.

1917 Efron joins the army. Daughter Irina born.

1918 Writes *Snowstorm,* and a play, *Knave of Hearts.*

1920 Irina dies of starvation in an orphanage.

1921 After not hearing from Efron for three years, learns he is alive. *Mileposts* published.

1922 To Berlin, where she unites with husband after four years. Begins romantic correspondence with Boris Pasternak. Plays and novels published in Russia. Moves to Czechoslovakia.

1923 *Psyche* and *Craft* published in Berlin. Affair with Rodzevich.

1925 Son Mur born. *The Ratcatcher.* Moves to Paris.
1926 Extended correspondence with Pasternak and Rilke.
1928 *After Russia*, last book published in her lifetime.
1934 Efron works for NKVD front organization.
1937 Daughter Ariadna (Alya) returns to Soviet Union. Efron implicated in murder of former Soviet agent, flees to Moscow. Marina interrogated by French police.
1939 At urging of family, moves back to Soviet Union.
1941 Evacuated to Elabuga. Hangs herself there.

Love. Betrayal. Exile. Death. Language. Country. Loss.

Up to the age of four I told the truth. After that, I must have come to my senses. If you're a good girl, grandpa will bring you a banana.

In the Pontic Swamps, Mithridates lost seven elephants and one eye.

I am not who I am, and the horse isn't mine.

To name is to take apart, to separate the self from the object. I never name anybody, ever.

The three ponds, her obsession with drowning, dying. The stolen apricots, betrayal, guilt. The gingerbread house, a sweet fantasy in which lies danger.

The creative state is a state of enchantment. At the top of the cliff is the Devil's white tower.

Standing in the enchanted circle of the garden of one's loneliness. Repeatedly inserting and removing a mandarin orange from her muff.

The Vurdalak gnaws my bones.

The dancer's task is to forget having known substance.

A staircase. I have been to invisible cities. How many fingers is God holding up? He has gathered the wind in his fists.

Two years after her death, her son told a friend that in her last months Marina had completely lost her mind. But at the time, he had little sympathy for her. It was only later that he realized that by then, his mother was made of pure suffering.

Erase everything you have written, said Mandelstam, but keep the notes in the margin.

Queens

I wonder if I have been changed in the night?
– Lewis Carroll, *Alice's Adventures In Wonderland*

CHARACTER & SETTING

ALICE – a girl of 16, who sits at a wooden table, shuffling an old pack of playing cards.

(**ALICE**, *a girl of 16, sits at an old wooden table, shuffling an old pack of playing cards which she perhaps uses to illustrate what she's saying.*)

ALICE. I've always known they were alive, ever since my father gave me an old pack of playing cards when I was a little girl. Watch out for the face cards, he said. Be careful they don't bite you. I used hide in the greenhouse in the back garden and look at the cards over and over again, and after a while they started talking to me. Now I know all their secrets.

The Queen of Hearts loves the Jack of Spades hopelessly, relentlessly, but all he can think about is the Queen of Diamonds. That is her tragedy.

The Queen of Diamonds is rich, she has everything, but nothing makes her happy. It's all emptiness. That is her sorrow. She enjoys teasing the Jack of Spades and making him angry. He has a rather bad temper, inherited from his father, which he unsuccessfully tries to hide with a smile. She really fancies the Jack of Clubs, who is quieter and more reflective, and doesn't want her. He thinks she's two dimensional. She wonders if he's right, and feels all empty inside.

The Queen of Spades is the bringer of Death to all who love her. She says the Queen of Diamonds is shallow and selfish and although very beautiful should probably be killed. They all want the Queen of Spades, but they're all afraid of her. She's very dangerous, especially in the game of Hearts. In the game of Hearts she is the card of death.

I used to play Hearts with my father. My father taught me to play. My father always wins.

The Jack of Clubs is in love with the Queen of Hearts, who's in love with the Jack of Spades, who's in love with the Queen of Diamonds, who's in love with the Queen of Spades, but doesn't know it. In her fantasies, the Queen of Spades kills the Jack of Diamonds while having sex. She cuts his throat.

The Queen of Clubs is melancholy. She has a sorrow she cannot reveal. She will never tell who she loves. But nobody cares.

The Jack of Hearts fucks anything that moves and loves nobody. He is the happiest of the cards because he has no morals, and just enough brains not to give a shit. When he's old, he'll be a fat, drunken pig like his father, the King of Hearts.

The problem with the Queen of Hearts is that she loves too much. She's a fool. She's always in love. The Queen of Spades says nobody can love chastely, not even the dead. She tells them it's all a game.

It does feel like that, says the Queen of Clubs. As if we are being played by someone, shuffled and played again and again in different combinations. And each shuffling of the cards brings such devastation. Relationships are ripped apart. We find ourselves pressed intimately next to strangers. One pressing into our back. And us pressed into someone's back. It seems almost as if the object of this game is to lose. The way you win is to lose. But we don't know the rules. We're only the playing cards. We are just the device through which the game is played. We can be replaced at any time by a newer, cleaner, less frayed and soiled version of ourselves.

When they're depressed, the Queens sit around and paint each other's toenails. Which is a surprise, because on the cards, they don't seem to have any toes. But there's lots to people you can't see just from looking. There's always something in them that's just out of the picture.

Who invents these games? Who makes these rules? And why are we forced to play them? The Queen of Diamonds thinks she knows. But she doesn't know. Nobody knows. You can't know if you're inside the game. And to go outside the game is to die. To be chewed up by the dog, or lost forever in the sofa cushions.

That sounds horrible. And it is horrible. But it's their life. And then we're shuffled and put in a drawer and we sit in the dark for days or weeks or months and it's so lonely.

Looking at the cards is like looking in the mirror. The King of Spades looks very much like my father.

At night when I lie in bed I can hear the sound of somebody shuffling cards in another room. Maybe it's God and the Devil, playing Hearts. And I'm just one of the cards.

Sometimes at night I dream that I'm one of them. Somebody comes to my bed in the middle of the night in the dark and does things to me. I close my eyes and pretend it's the Jack of Diamonds. But when I open my eyes I can see it's the King of Spades.

The rules of this game are different.

The Kings are the fathers of the Queens, and they have sexual intercourse with them. The Jacks are the brothers of the Queens and they also have sexual intercourse with them. And the Queens are raped by the other Kings and love the other Jacks. It's like a really dirty soap opera going on there in that pack of cards. And it keeps changing every time you shuffle.

And sometimes the Queens have intercourse with cards that don't have faces, especially the Aces, who are big and brutal. But what does it matter, in the end? In the end, the game is over, and they put you in the drawer and forget about you.

I want to be the Queen of Spades. They all desire and fear the Queen of Spades. They're all drawn into the bathtub drain of her soul, where everybody will drown. They're drawn to her cruelty. It makes her strong. To be strong, you've got to be cruel. My father taught me that.

One night when he was drunk he said to me, you know what they do to little girls who talk too much? They cut their throats with a playing card.

And I thought about that for years. And I wondered if it was true. I wondered if you could cut a man's throat with a playing card? And it turns out you can, if you just get him drunk enough first. Off with his head, said the Queen.

My father had a lot of blood in him.

That's why they put me in this place. But I don't care. I have the cards to keep me company. I live inside the deck of cards now, in my head. But the thing is, you've got to keep shuffling the cards. You've got to keep shuffling the cards or you start thinking and you lose the game. You're all right as long as you keep shuffling the cards. Just keep shuffling the cards.

(She shuffles the cards. The light fades on her and goes out.)

The Wood Where Things Have No Names

She very soon came to an open field, with a wood on the other side of it: it looked much darker than the last wood, and Alice felt a little timid about going into it. However, on second thoughts, she made up her mind to go on: "for I certainly won't go back," she thought to herself, and this was the only way to the Eighth Square. "This must be the wood, she said thoughtfully to herself," where things have no names."

– Lewis Carroll, *Through The Looking-Glass*

CHARACTER

JADE – a young woman

SETTING

A garden in winter

With thanks to Jade Lane, for whose reading series in New York it was written and first heard in December 2013.

(**JADE**, *a young woman, in a garden in winter.*)

JADE. So she goes through the mirror to the room on the other side where everything is reversed and time behaves strangely. The White Queen remembers the future. And there's a little shop, with a ticking clock, but whenever you try to look at any particular spot on the shelf, it seems empty, although everything around it is full, and yet when you look up, or down, or to either side, the emptiness moves with you, and the White Queen turns to a leg of mutton and then she's peering over the edge of the soup tureen, and I'm in a row boat with a sheep wrapped in a shawl, and she's trying to tell me something but I can't make out what she's saying. My father read me this in a tree house a very long time ago, and now I dream about it. Only it's all jumbled up. We are the Red King's dream. Things are not what they seem.

It's been arranged somehow so that what you want to remember you forget, and what you'd like to forget you remember, so gradually, over time, all the good things disappear and only the bad things stay. The problem with going home for the holidays is that the place you remember isn't there because it never existed except in your head and your family isn't real, it's like everybody there is like a bad actor impersonating the people you remember. Something is wrong. Something is always wrong. They've somehow rearranged the furniture while you were gone. They've taken the house apart and put it together again but everything's not quite right. And everybody's got the wrong masks on. It's the other side of the looking-glass.

The thing about betrayal. The thing about betrayal is that it destroys the imaginary world you've created in your head, the world in which you are actually loved. It forces you to see it wasn't real. Nothing good is real. The test of whether anything is real or not is if it makes you happy. If it makes you happy then it isn't real. And of course, if I could have remembered the future like the White Queen I would have known what would happen, what is bound to happen when you allow yourself to embrace the illusion that you are loved. How many impossible things can you believe before breakfast? Six at least. But as the day progresses, darkness gathers, and one by one the impossible things you believed are transformed to lizards and fish and playing cards.

The White Knight rescues her from the Red Knight but both of them keep falling off their horses onto their heads and in the end being rescued from one unreal square on the checkerboard only brings you to another unreal square. You're still lost in the woods, and everybody around you is mad.

One might persuade one's self to forgive him, of course. Could one? I don't know if one could or not. Would it really be forgiving, or would it just be returning once again to the previous delusion in which you imagined you were loved? Or perhaps instead one's destination is the wood where things have no names. Where one does not say, I love you. Or, that person loves me. I am not this person, with this name, in this body. I am somebody else entirely, somebody I can't remember, because I can only remember the future, and I have no future. There is none. There is only a half-remembered fragmentary past in which your father reads to you in a tree house and you're perfectly happy.

So one has loved. One has allowed one's self to participate in the delusion that one is loved. When perhaps one secretly knew all along that the object of one's love was, although very appealing in many ways, not to be trusted. Because the object of one's love is always somebody else. It's never who you think you love. It's someone you've cast in the role of a person you used to love, who's gone now. Someone who used to read to you in a tree house. Being in love is like writing a play in which everybody is miscast, but you don't realize it until half way through the second act.

So here is the question. Does she forgive the impostor who has betrayed her, and resume pretending this person loves her? He is often forgiven, although to him she is merely a leg of mutton. He is the master of amiable breakups. He knows how to keep his options open. He is the Knave of Hearts. Or does she move on to a future she does not remember, and can't envision, except as a meaningless series of ongoing humiliations, betrayals, and despair? Does she go home for the holidays, to a place which is no longer home, to see people who are strangers to her now? Or does she enter the wood where things have no names? A place from which there is perhaps no exit.

It's beginning to snow. In the wood where things have no names, there is no future. There is no past. There is only a perfect whiteness, like snow falling. You look in the mirror and nobody is there.

(The light fades on her and goes out.)

Pentecost

When thou hearest the sound of a going in the tops of the mulberry trees, that then thou shall bestir thyself: for then shall the Lord go out before thee, to smite the host of the Philistines.
– 2 Samuel 5:24

What love is so deep as hate? ... There is no madness in my flesh, but only the vehemence of the desire that has eaten me up.
– Rudyard Kipling, *Dray Wara Yow Dee*

The sun shall be turned into darkness, and the moon into blood ...
– Acts 2:20

CHARACTERS

EGG ROOKS – 29
DORRY SHAY – 19
JACK PENTECOST – 33

SETTING & TIME

A rainy night in the year 1880. A deserted windmill deep in the east Ohio woods. The set is mostly darkness, except for the dim light of a small invisible downstage fire

*(Sound of wind and rain, and the creaking of an old windmill. Lights up on **JACK PENTECOST**, sitting before the flickering light of an invisible downstage fire in a deserted windmill in the east Ohio woods. **EGG ROOKS** appears upstage, with an old brown rucksack.)*

EGG. I saw your fire. Thought maybe you wouldn't mind if I came in out of the rain. That's a powerful lot of wind and rain going on out there. I'll just put my bag down here to dry off. I got mud on me like a pig in slop. You come in out of the rain too, did you? I don't figure anybody lives in this old windmill, if you don't count the rats. Don't look to me like anybody lives anywhere around here. I don't even rightly know where I am. Don't usually get lost, but I guess that's because I stay home most of the time. Which is not as smart as it sounds, since I live at the dump. You grow up at the dump, there's a certain stink you can't get off you, no matter how much you wash. Even if other people can't smell it, you can.

*(Getting a better look at **JACK**.)*

I know you.

JACK. I don't think so.

EGG. You're Jack Pentecost.

JACK. I'm not anybody.

EGG. Well, I'll be damned. Fancy coming across Jack Pentecost, on a night like this, in an old windmill in the middle of nowhere. Ain't life mysterious?

(Sitting down by the fire.)

It's bad luck to set a fire in a windmill, Jack. But I'm glad you did. On a night like this, I'd sit down with the Devil, just to get warm. You know, you're famous in our parts. Yes you are. You're quite a preacher. I seen you once. It was very impressive. Kinda like the circus. You was more entertaining than monkeys in a clown car. When I was just a little fella, my Uncle Scooter used to make a speech before he'd cut the heads off chickens. Your show was kind of like that. I went there with this girl I was powerfully attached to. I'm not real big on religion, myself, but this girl, she was an unusual sort of a girl. She had visions, or some sort of thing like that. Thought she did, anyway. Used to tell me her dreams. She had some real corkers.

DORRY. *(Appearing from the upstage shadows, from another time and place, barefoot, in an old wedding dress, moving into the flickering light.)* I dreamed I was riding on a train late one night, and I was reading the Bible, that chapter about the wind going in the mulberry trees, and the wind started turning the pages, to the part about Pentecost, and I felt these two strong hands reaching around my neck from behind.

> *(Putting her hands on **JACK**'s shoulders, on either side of his neck.)*

JACK. I think you've got me confused with somebody else.

EGG. Oh, I don't think so. I got a psychopathic memory, which is not necessarily an advantage in life.

DORRY. And he said to me, as he was pressing his hands into my neck, in my dream, while the wind was going in the mulberry trees, he said, If your mirror is broken, look into still water.

JACK. But be careful you don't fall in.

DORRY. But be careful you don't fall in, he said.

EGG. There's a lot of things you'd just as soon forget when you grow up at the dump.

JACK. *(Reaching up to cover her hands with his.)* I knew a girl once who fell into a mirror and never came out.

EGG. My Uncle Scooter, he ran the junkyard by the dump. Him and Aunt Aggie raised me after I found my Daddy at the bottom of a hole with his head pointing in the wrong direction. He had fallen into a serious state of disrepair after kicking Mama down the steps, drunk himself into oblivion and stepped into a sink hole. But my Uncle Scooter, he said, Egg, don't you never be ashamed of your Daddy, just because he was a drunken, murdering jackass that kicked my sister down the stairs so he could fornicate with my other sister. You honor your Daddy's memory by running the best goddamned junkyard in Pendragon County. We always had pretty high standards, for people who live at the dump. I didn't want just any girl. I wanted a girl I'd never even be tempted to kick down the stairs. And I knew right away, the minute I set eyes on her, that this girl was different. She was special.

DORRY. Take off your clothes, he said, or the Lord will snap your neck like a chicken bone.

EGG. Like what Aunt Aggie used to call fey. Aunt Aggie was Uncle Scooter's other sister. The one my Daddy fornicated with in his deep remorse after he kicked my Mama down the basement steps and broke her neck. She said my Mama was fey. And this girl, she was like that. She could see things other people couldn't. She was a little bit touched in the head.

DORRY. I wanted to scream, but I couldn't make a sound.

EGG. My Uncle Scooter warned me never to get sweet on a woman, or trust a woman, or have any damned thing to do with a woman.

DORRY. And I was trembling, in my dream.

EGG. Of course, my Uncle Scooter had married my Aunt Messy, who was both stupid and crazy, and he used to express his disappointment by getting rip roaring drunk and beating us with a horse whip, so I never took what he said as Gospel.

DORRY. Just shaking and shaking.

EGG. Uncle Scooter died a war hero. He didn't have to go, but he enlisted in the Union Army, either to get away from Aunt Messy or the smell of the dump, one or the other. And he did, too. Stood up to look at a bird and a cannon ball took off his head.

DORRY. Shuddering and shuddering.

EGG. But I never seen anybody with eyes like that girl. Like a blue eyed snake.

DORRY. It scared me, that dream.

EGG. Every time I hear the wind going through the mulberry trees, I think about her. Don't know where she come from. Just showed up one day.

DORRY. How I got to this town was, the train was moving through a herd of pigs, and the conductor was coming, and I didn't have a ticket, so I got off, and I liked it here.

EGG. Got herself a waitress job at the bowling alley, slept in the attic where they had the old piano from the church got warped in the flood where mice made a nest, and a mess of trunks and mirrors from when the vaudeville folk used to stay there when they played the Odessa Theatre around the corner when the bowling alley was a boarding house and they'd skip town without paying because you can't trust show folk any further than you can kick a dead moose.

DORRY. Once them pigs moved on, the whole town smelled like fresh bread and fried chicken.

EGG. She was the worst damned waitress God ever made, but she was so pleasant to look at, nobody cared. Something about her. You just wanted to hold onto her and not let go.

(*JACK's hands are tightening on DORRY's.*)

DORRY. (*Pulling her hands away from JACK's, then sitting down between them, in front of the fire.*) When I was a little girl, my Mama and me used to travel from town to town, running from the Devil and drinking water out of rain barrels.

JACK. You can't run away from the Devil. Wherever you run to, he's already there, waiting in the mirror.

DORRY. I know. Because now and then I could still smell him. The Devil smells like burning leaves. I can smell him lurking in a box of tomatoes, like some kind of poison spider that follows me around. It got my Mama. She went berserk and fell on the railroad track. Locomotive cut her in three different pieces. Found her head in a mud puddle looking kind of surprised. All she left me was her wedding dress.

EGG. Once I got a look at that girl, I started going into town and eating at the bowling alley, which was a sacrifice on my part, because I'd rather stick my head up a cow's ass than go bowling, and the food at that place tasted like fried dog feet. But I went there every night, just so I could watch her. We was starting to get pretty friendly when you come to town, and she wanted to see your show real bad, so I took her out there. You was speaking in tongues.

JACK. BackwardsLackawannacopperhorse wooddresserclownpunch bluerecordblack widowpussyhopper. Deathwatch beetletrees.

EGG. And I could see her getting so excited, her eyes so big, listening to you.

JACK. Lipwhistle wetmouth pastasucker lipscreamer.

EGG. And before I knew it, damned if she didn't start speaking in tongues, too.

DORRY. Flibbergibbet flicktummy wackadoodle bloomersop.

EGG. And there was the two of you, in front of God and the Devil and the whole town, just jabbering away at each other in tongues, like you actually knew what the hell each other was talking about.

JACK. Sweethoney tonguewash babyladle humpsister.

DORRY. Gooseflesh glockenspieler doomeylord doomey doomey.

EGG. It was the damnedest crock of bullshit I ever heard in my life.

JACK. Pentecost celebrates the descent of the Holy Spirit.

DORRY. It comes through the hole, he said.

JACK. It comes through the hole. The Holy Spirit hole. A small, round hole in a church the Holy Spirit comes through. Like the hole in the wall under the mulberry tree where Pyramus met Thisbe. As performed by the rude mechanicals in the play within the play.

DORRY. Uh huh.

JACK. Shakespeare. Midsummer. And before that, Ovid.

DORRY. Okay.

JACK. It's part of the Pentecost services.

DORRY. Like your name.

JACK. Of course, that was profane love, and turned out badly.

EGG. I'll bet you know something about profane love, don't you, Jack? I'll bet you put your finger in a lot of holes, every new town you come to.

JACK. I'm investigating the mysteries of the Holy Trinity.

EGG. I'll bet you are.

JACK. The world is full of signs written in foreign tongues. Everyone has sinned. But anyone can be saved. If they have the right dictionary.

DORRY. I want to be saved. Save me.

EGG. My rucksack is all wet. I'm gonna just move it closer to the fire. You like my rucksack, Jack? I brought it all the way from home, when I come looking for you.

DORRY. In my dream, I was naked, and the train was rocking back and forth.

JACK. Why would you be looking for me?

DORRY. And something was on top of me, and I couldn't hardly breathe.

EGG. I come for some spiritual guidance.

DORRY. And when I opened my eyes, I saw it was the Devil, reflected in pieces of a broken mirror on an old rug in the attic by the piano.

JACK. I don't think I can help you.

DORRY. And I thought, this is a dream.

EGG. Oh, don't sell yourself short, Jack.

DORRY. This is more real than my life.

EGG. I mean, you're a man of the world. And a man of God. I'm just some dumb shit kicker who lives at the dump.

DORRY. And I knew then, in my dream, that the train was going to Hell. But I didn't care.

EGG. It's about that girl.

JACK. I don't know anything about women.

EGG. But you've had a lot of women, haven't you, Jack?

JACK. The more you have, the less you know.

EGG. She's the sort of a girl you just can't get out of your head. I used to dream about making love to that girl with the wind going in the mulberry trees. Just smelling that girl's hair was a religious experience.

JACK. A naked girl, helpless in your arms, is a holy object.

EGG. And in my dream, while I was doing it to her, she was speaking in tongues.

DORRY. Everywhen nothingisn't skinkiss losthorses.

EGG. I was made stupid by her beauty. It blinded me.

JACK. Women are fascinated by their power to hurt us.

DORRY. Like that time, out in the peach orchard.

JACK. Which is why the more successful among us have learned to get out of town first.

DORRY. When I thought I could feel somebody breathing on my neck.

JACK. If you hurt a woman, she will always love you.

DORRY. And I didn't know if it was God or the Devil.

JACK. It's God's dirty little secret.

DORRY. But whoever it was, I knew I liked it.

EGG. Not that I got any illusions about women, or anything else.

DORRY. I liked the feeling of danger.

EGG. I know that rats and whores is all there is.

DORRY. The feeling of sin and holiness all mixed together.

EGG. The men are all rats and the women are all whores.

JACK. There is no ecstasy without violation.

EGG. The voice told me. I always did hear it. I'd lay on my belly in the night at the dump and listen. Maybe it was the Devil. Maybe it was my Uncle Scooter's voice.

JACK. No passion without betrayal.

EGG. I bet you heard a lot of things stranger than that, Jack.

JACK. As in the garden, with a kiss.

EGG. In the midst of all your wanderings, while you was investigating the mystery of the trinity and that magic hole, speaking in tongues.

JACK. When the voice comes out, it's not me any more.

DORRY. I just couldn't stop shuddering.

JACK. Something rushes out of me. I don't know what it means.

EGG. Rip a man's heart out, tear it into shreds with her teeth, fry it up in a pan.

JACK. God is broadcasting. I'm just the radio. Which is an invention from the future God showed me in a vision.

EGG. That's a woman for you.

JACK. At least I like to tell myself it's God.

EGG. Love comes into your head, there's just plain lunacy after that. Nothing else.

DORRY. He washed my feet.

JACK. When I'm dead, the radio is broken.

DORRY. He washed my whole body. He kissed my whole body. He licked my whole body like a cat washing a kitten.

JACK. But the broadcast continues.

DORRY. Are you washed in the blood of the lamb?

JACK. Other radios pick it up.

DORRY. I could feel it going in me. The Holy Spirit. It entered right into me. In the peach orchard. Up in the attic.

EGG. So imagine how I felt when I looked through the window one night and saw you violating her up against the piano in the attic, above the bowling alley.

DORRY. We worshipped together in the upper room. With the bird cages and the old cracked mirrors and the smell of the old piano.

JACK. Through a glass, darkly.

DORRY. Like the wind going in the mulberry trees.

JACK. A small, circular opening.

DORRY. Speaking in tongues and sweating like pigs.

JACK. But when any two make the beast, there is always a third party present.

DORRY. *(Staring into the fire, hypnotized by the memory.)* He split me in two, like a pomegranate. And my juice poured out all over him, like sweet communion wine.

JACK. God is always present.

EGG. I seen it through the window.

JACK. He likes to watch.

DORRY. The moon all turned to blood.

JACK. In my dream, night after night, a gigantic moth comes to suck out my soul. The flapping of its wings. How many have I violated?

DORRY. Left me there all weak and trembling.

JACK. The innocent. The hungry. The lost.

DORRY. One of the damned. Or the saved. I don't know which.

JACK. Sucking everything out until there was nothing.

DORRY. Washed in the blood of the lamb.

JACK. And the attic in which I violated this girl was full of old trunks and mirrors. And she wanted to show me her mother's wedding dress. She opened a trunk, and moths flew out, white moths flew out, and I saw the

Devil looking at me from the mirrors, and I knew I had to get away from that place.

EGG. So after you was done with her, I went in through the door you left open. And right up the steps to that attic.

JACK. Blood of the lamb.

EGG. She'd put on that old wedding dress.

DORRY. I was cold, after.

EGG. She looked so innocent, and lost.

DORRY. I felt so empty inside.

EGG. So beautiful I could hardly breathe.

DORRY. Like he'd hollowed me out until I was nothing.

EGG. And for a moment, I just felt all this tenderness wash over me.

DORRY. Eaten me out like moths.

EGG. She was startled to see me, at first.

DORRY. Then something come up the steps and out of the darkness.

EGG. I tried to tell her I'd forgive her. I'd marry her. Even after I saw her sin and all.

DORRY. Get away from me. Don't touch me.

EGG. I guess I didn't say it very well.

DORRY. Don't touch me.

EGG. I ain't never been very good at talking about my feelings.

DORRY. Peeking in the windows. You smell like the dump. I don't want you. The Devil's going to come back and take me with him, on the train to Hell.

EGG. But lucky for me, I happened to bring along my Uncle Scooter's hand ax, that he used to cut the heads off chickens with.

JACK. Do you hear that flapping sound?

EGG. And then the voice told me what I had to do.

DORRY. Washed in the blood of the lamb.

EGG. I'm sure glad I found you, Jack. Because I brought you a present. I got it right here in my rucksack. You want to see what I got for you in my rucksack, Jack?

DORRY. The saved and the damned are the same.

EGG. Something to keep you company on a cold rainy night in a windmill. Somebody to talk to when you get lonesome. I brought it all the way from the bowling alley. I'll give you a hint, Jack. It's real pretty. But it ain't no bowling ball.

> *(Sound of the wind and the rain and the creaking of the windmill as the light fades on them and goes out.)*

Lamp Post

*The Lamp Post stands
in the middle of the forest
in the Lantern Waste
and marks the portal
to the other place.*

CHARACTERS

BEN – late twenties
BRITTANY – twenties

SETTING & TIME

An upstairs apartment in a Midwestern college town in the late 1970s.

(Sound of loud pounding on the door in the dark.)

BRITTANY. *(From outside the door.)* Is this the Crisis Center?

BEN. *(Sleepy, in the dark.)* What?

BRITTANY. *(Pounding on the door.)* Is this the Crisis Center?

BEN. No.

BRITTANY. *(Pounding on the door.)* Why is the door locked? Is this the Crisis Center or what?

BEN. This is not the Crisis Center.

BRITTANY. Yes it is.

BEN. No it's not.

BRITTANY. *(Pounding on the door.)* Open the door. This is a crisis.

BEN. *(Turning on the light, looking at the clock.)* The Crisis Center is next door.

BRITTANY. I want the Crisis Center.

BEN. It's next door.

BRITTANY. Next door to what?

BEN. Next door.

BRITTANY. There's nothing next door. What door?

BEN. You've got to go down the steps.

BRITTANY. What?

BEN. *(Making his way groggily to the door. He's wearing a tee shirt and boxer shorts.)* Go down the steps, out the door, turn right, and go next door.

BRITTANY. What's the matter with you people? You're supposed to be the Crisis Center.

BEN. I'm not the Crisis Center.

BRITTANY. You've got to help me. I'm in trouble out here.

BEN. Go down the steps and out the door.

BRITTANY. I can't go back out there. Please let me in. Please. Please. Oh, God, please. I'm scared. I'm so scared. Somebody's after me.

BEN. All right.

>   (**BEN** *opens the door.*)

BRITTANY. *(Rushing in.)* Close the door.

BEN. *(Looking out the door.)* Is somebody out there?

BRITTANY. *(Pushing him out of her way and slamming the door shut.)* Get out of the way, asshole. I told you to shut the door.

>   *(She stands there with her back to the door, panting. Looking at him.)*

You don't have any pants on.

BEN. I was in bed.

BRITTANY. What the hell kind of Crisis Center is this?

BEN. This is not the Crisis Center.

BRITTANY. What are you, some kind of pervert?

BEN. I'm not any kind of pervert.

BRITTANY. They let people like you walk around the Crisis Center without your pants on?

BEN. I'm not walking around the Crisis Center. I'm walking around in my apartment.

BRITTANY. You live at the Crisis Center?

BEN. I live in my apartment.

BRITTANY. Then why don't you go back there?

BEN. I am there. This is my apartment.

BRITTANY. What happened to the Crisis Center?

BEN. It's down stairs next door.

BRITTANY. No it's not.

BEN. Who's after you?

BRITTANY. I don't know. Did you see them?

BEN. I didn't see anybody.

BRITTANY. Then what are you talking about?

BEN. You said somebody was after you.

BRITTANY. I thought they were.

BEN. Do you want me to call the police?

BRITTANY. No. Don't call the police. I've got weed in my pocket.

BEN. Great. Do you want me to call the Crisis Center?

BRITTANY. Why would you want to call the Crisis Center?

BEN. I don't know. Why are you here?

BRITTANY. Because I'm having a crisis. Why the fuck do you think I'm here?

BEN. Because you thought this was the Crisis Center.

BRITTANY. It is the Crisis Center.

BEN. No, it's not.

BRITTANY. You are the worst Crisis Center person I've ever seen in my life.

BEN. I'm not a Crisis Center person.

BRITTANY. Then what are you doing here?

BEN. I'm just trying to get some sleep.

BRITTANY. Then why did you lure me in here?

BEN. I didn't lure you in here. You said you were in trouble.

BRITTANY. I am in trouble.

BEN. Then I'm calling the police.

BRITTANY. Stay away from that phone. It might be bugged. They can do things like that.

BEN. Who can?

BRITTANY. I don't know. Could you put your pants on?

BEN. Sure. Why not?

(He looks for his pants.)

BRITTANY. Do you have something to drink?

BEN. I have water.

BRITTANY. No, not water. They put stuff in the water.

BEN. *(Finding his pants, putting them on.)* I've got Squirt.

BRITTANY. Squirt? You've got Squirt?

BEN. Yes. Do you want a Squirt?

BRITTANY. Is that some kind of sexual reference? Because I don't like that sort of talk.

BEN. Squirt is a soft drink.

BRITTANY. You make one funny move, buster, and I'm leaving.

BEN. How about if I stand on my head?

BRITTANY. Why would you want to stand on your head? God, you're weird. This is why I don't like to hang out at the Crisis Center. There's a lot of weird people there. Are you alone here?

BEN. No. J. Edgar Hoover is in the bathroom, putting something in the water.

BRITTANY. Don't get snippy with me. I've just had a terrible experience.

BEN. And I'm having one right now. Did you escape from some sort of mental institution?

BRITTANY. No. Not recently. I was walking on the brick sidewalk by that long row of lamp posts down towards the campus, which I do every night, coming home from the library, and every night when I walk by this one lamp post the light goes out. None of the other lights. Just that one. And it's always the same one. It stays on until I get close to it and then it goes out. And then after I walk by, I look back and it comes on again. And it stays on.

BEN. So the bulb is going.

BRITTANY. No. That's the thing. It only does it for me. It's always perfectly fine until I go by. And I've watched other people go by and nothing happens. But when I go by, the light goes off. And then it won't come on again until I'm down the street. Don't you see what it means?

BEN. It means the bulb is going.

BRITTANY. It means that psychic energy is streaming out of my head and turning that light off.

BEN. No it doesn't.

BRITTANY. What other explanation could there be?

BEN. There's something wrong with the light.

BRITTANY. But it only happens with me.

BEN. You don't know that.

BRITTANY. But I watched.

BEN. How long did you watch?

BRITTANY. Are you calling me a liar?

BEN. No, I'm saying you don't know what the light does when you're not there.

BRITTANY. But it only does it when I'm there.

BEN. But you don't know that, because you're only there when you're there.

BRITTANY. Of course I'm only there when I'm there. How could I be there when I'm not there? What kind of logic is that?

BEN. It's apophenia.

BRITTANY. What did you call me?

BEN. Apophenia. It's seeing meaningful patterns or connections in random data. People confuse randomness with meaningfulness because we've evolved to look for patterns. That's how we make sense of the world.

BRITTANY. How can I see a pattern if it's not there?

BEN. Random data can contain accidental patterns. Patterns that don't mean anything.

BRITTANY. But who decides the patterns don't mean anything?

BEN. Nobody decides. They do or they don't.

BRITTANY. But how do you know?

BEN. By observation over time.

BRITTANY. I've been observing over time.

BEN. Not enough observation and not enough time.

BRITTANY. Well, what am I supposed to do? Sit there all night staring at the lamp post?

BEN. That would be a start.

BRITTANY. That would be insane.

BEN. Well, yes, but if you wanted to get a big enough sampling of evidence to draw a conclusion –

BRITTANY. You're saying it's a coincidence.

BEN. That's what I'm saying.

BRITTANY. But coincidence can be meaningful. Synchronicity. Right? Isn't that what synchronicity is? Meaningful coincidence?

BEN. That's what Jung says it is, but in fact it's probably just another example of apophenia.

BRITTANY. So you're smarter than Jung too, huh? You're smarter than everybody.

BEN. I'm just saying there might be a more sensible explanation for why the light goes out than jumping to the conclusion that brain waves come zapping out of your head when you go by. That's a delusion of reference.

BRITTANY. Where are you getting all these fancy terms? Are you making them up? You're not a writer, are you? Because I hate writers. This campus is so damned full of writers there's enough bullshit in this town to fertilize China.

BEN. A delusion of reference is the belief that random phenomena have a deep personal significance to a person.

BRITTANY. You don't believe that anything can have a deep personal significance to a person?

BEN. Of course. But not random phenomena.

BRITTANY. But you're just calling it random. You're presuming there's no connection. You're taking it upon yourself to decide for me what has deep personal significance for me and what doesn't. What a smug, arrogant son of a bitch. You are a writer, aren't you?

BEN. That has nothing to do with what we're talking about.

BRITTANY. That damned writer's workshop draws every self-obsessed loser in the universe to this place. You want to talk about people who have an irrational view of their own personal significance? What a bunch of neurotic gas bags. I used to work in the library, and while I was supposed to be shelving books I was up in the stacks reading these thesis novels from the fiction workshop. What a bunch of shit. They're all the same. Safe little sensitive precious pieces of minimalist self-referential bullshit, with maybe a little wry twist at the end, so subtle it's hardly even there. God. Hasn't anybody got any balls around here? This bland shit is supposed to be literature? It's hardly even writing. And then you all sit around and congratulate each other while secretly hating each other's guts and then go out and hire each other to teach the same sort of crap to other mediocre losers like yourself. It's like a black hole that swallows up talent and shits mediocrity. God forbid anything here should ever have any fucking deep personal significance. God forbid anything could actually mean anything. Oh, no. Let's call it apophenia or delusional reference or slap some other damned stupid label on it so we don't have to think about it any more. Because if the universe actually meant anything, it might mean that the fucking writer's workshop is just one big giant shit factory.

BEN. So is this part of your crisis or is it just bonus observations on your part?

BRITTANY. My crisis is that that goddamned light keeps blinking off when I walk by and doesn't come on again until I walk away, and it's freaking me out, because I think all kinds of crap is flying out of my head in all directions, and it's probably ruining my life, because I've noticed that people are attracted to me at first and then suddenly they back off and I never see them again.

BEN. And you don't think there could be some other explanation for that? Like that people decide you're insane because you think you've got some kind of a deeply significant cosmic connection to a lamp post?

BRITTANY. So you're saying there is no significance.

BEN. I'm saying the street light blinking has no significance.

BRITTANY. You're saying it can't be connected, that nothing is connected.

BEN. Some things are connected. Just not that.

BRITTANY. Because you say so?

BEN. Because there's no evidence.

BRITTANY. I saw it happen with my own eyes.

BEN. Look. I had a cat once. I put an old piece of railroad track at the bottom of the basement steps to hold the screen door shut, and she was walking by one day just as my father turned on his electric razor in the bathroom at the top of the steps.

BRITTANY. Why are we talking about your cat?

BEN. She happened to be sniffing the piece of railroad track just as the razor started to buzz, and it scared her. She jumped back and hissed at the track. She thought the piece of railroad track was making the buzzing noise. And for years afterwards, every time she went by that piece of railroad track keeping the screen door closed, she hissed at it. Do you see? She happened to put her nose on it right when the razor started buzzing, so she thought it made the noise. She imagined a relationship that wasn't the case because the buzzing and the sniffing happened at the same time. She presumed a cause and effect relationship when in fact the two incidents were random.

BRITTANY. So you're saying I'm as dumb as your cat.

BEN. No, my cat was very smart.

BRITTANY. So you're saying I'm dumber than your cat.

BEN. I'm saying you both experienced events that happened simultaneously and presumed, falsely but perhaps understandably, that the events were related, when in fact they were not.

BRITTANY. It's not the same thing at all.

BEN. It's an analogy.

BRITTANY. I have nothing but pity for people like you.

BEN. Why?

BRITTANY. Because you've got to explain everything away. You're so afraid of learning anything new that you've got to have contempt for other people's experience. You've got to reduce everything to something you already know. Well, you don't know everything.

BEN. I didn't say I knew everything.

BRITTANY. There's all kinds of things going on in this world you don't have a clue about.

BEN. I'm sure there are.

BRITTANY. You're belittling the significance of my personal experience just to make yourself feel superior.

BEN. No I'm not.

BRITTANY. The world is a forest of symbols.

BEN. Well, maybe, in a sense, the way an artist would look at it. But –

BRITTANY. Before we could see germs, people like you made fun of the whole idea that germs could exist, right?

BEN. I didn't personally make fun of germs.

BRITTANY. The Pope wouldn't look through the telescope at the moon because he thought he already knew everything about the universe, didn't he?

BEN. I'm not talking about the Pope.

BRITTANY. I'm making an analogy. If you can make an analogy, I can make an analogy.

BEN. But you're making a false analogy.

BRITTANY. You're comparing me to your cat and a piece of old railroad track but I'm making a false analogy?

BEN. Look. It's very late. I'm tired. Is your crisis over?

BRITTANY. No, my crisis isn't over. You're making it worse.

BEN. Why is this a crisis, anyway? I mean, so what if you have this magical power to make one street light go out when you walk by it? Why should that upset you?

BRITTANY. Because it scares me. The power scares me. I don't know how to use this power. What if I get mad at somebody and it makes them step in front of a bus or something?

BEN. Did you ever get mad at anybody who stepped in front of a bus?

BRITTANY. I got mad at my grandfather and he dropped dead.

BEN. Once again, unless you put arsenic in his oatmeal, you're imagining a relationship between two completely unrelated things.

BRITTANY. But how do you know for sure? Just because nobody has figured out an experiment they can repeat over and over again and make the same thing happen, like dropping a bowling ball off a bell tower or something, doesn't mean there isn't any connection. All kinds of things are connected that we don't know about. That's what science is. And that's what art is, too, right? Making connections between things that other people didn't make before. Which is why your stupid writer's workshop stories really, really suck the big one. Because they're not making connections that other people haven't made before. They're only making connections that other people have already made. Somebody is going along and sneering at anybody who does anything different and making them stop, and the result is a drab, dead, lifeless, worthless slop. It's dead. And you're dead. All of you people are dead. You think you're creating something but you're not creating anything. Nothing is being created here and nothing of any value is being learned. Because it's all just the scared mediocre puke of scared mediocre people. And meanwhile, all around us, there's this whole universe of unexplained and terrifying things that all of you are too damned full of yourselves to even acknowledge the possibility of. And it's people like you who run the world.

BEN. Writers? Writers run the world?

BRITTANY. Mediocrities. People with skills just a little above average end up running everything, because that's what they're good at. They don't make anything. They don't create anything of any real value. They just like telling people what to do and feeling superior to anybody who actually uses their brain. All my life I've seen this. People telling me, no, no, Brittany, you can't do this, you can't say that, you can't think that. My grandfather was like that.

BEN. Well, not any more, because apparently you killed him with your mind.

BRITTANY. What a horrible thing to say.

BEN. I didn't say that. You said that.

BRITTANY. I come to the Crisis Center for help, and instead I get accused of murdering my grandfather.

BEN. This is not the Crisis Center.

BRITTANY. Then why are you talking to me?

BEN. I thought you were in trouble.

BRITTANY. I am in trouble.

BEN. All this is about that one damned blinking street light?

BRITTANY. No, it's not just about the light. It's about everything. It's about my relationship to the world. I feel like I have so much stuff inside my brain that my head is going to explode. I feel like I could go over to Black's Gaslight Village and things would shoot out of my head and kill the peacocks.

BEN. What peacocks?

BRITTANY. At Black's Gaslight Village. I wanted to live there because they have peacocks walking around on the grounds, and I thought it would be nice, you know, to live among the peacocks, so I went over there to ask about renting a room, and I kept stepping on dead peacocks. There were dead peacocks everywhere.

BEN. Brittany, you didn't murder any peacocks.

BRITTANY. How do you know?

BEN. Because it was me. I like to sneak into Black's Gaslight Village in the middle of the night and brain peacocks with a baseball bat.

BRITTANY. Why would you do that?

BEN. I don't know. Something just comes over me. In fact, I'm starting to get the feeling right now.

BRITTANY. What the fuck are you talking about?

BEN. *(Going over to open the door.)* I'm not talking about anything, because it's four o'clock in the morning, and you're not here, you're actually at the Crisis Center, which is just down the steps and to your right.

BRITTANY. *(Rushing over, arms extended, frantic.)* DON'T OPEN THAT DOOR.

> *(She runs into him and slams the door shut, his back against it. Her face is against his chest. She's clutching him.)*

BEN. *(Instinctively putting his hands on her shoulders.)* I think you cracked a rib.

BRITTANY. *(Reacting to the touch. Backing away abruptly.)* GET YOUR GODDAMNED HANDS OFF ME. I'VE GOT A GUN.

BEN. You've got a gun?

BRITTANY. So just don't mess with me. I am so tired of everybody messing with me.

BEN. Where is this gun?

BRITTANY. In Pennsylvania.

BEN. You've got a gun in Pennsylvania.

BRITTANY. And I know how to use it, too. My grandfather taught me.

> *(Pause.)*

I'm so tired. You have no idea how tired I am.

BEN. Actually, I do.

BRITTANY. No. You don't know. Nobody knows. You're just some random guy. You have no significance whatsoever. And neither does anything else. Nothing means anything. Nothing has ever meant anything. Nothing ever will mean anything.

>   *(Sitting down on the bed in despair.)*

It's all just random.

>   *(Pause. She looks at her hands.)*

This isn't the Crisis Center, is it?

>   *(**BEN** looks at her. She looks very sad, small, and lost. Pause.)*

BEN. I don't know. Maybe.

>   *(She looks at him. The light fades on them and goes out.)*

Zombie Radio

CHARACTERS

MEREDITH CHERRY – 17
JIM RAINEY – 18

SETTING & TIME

A sofa in the living room of a brick house at 405 Armitage Avenue in Armitage, a small town in east Ohio, in the autumn of the year 1954. Meredith and Jim are sitting on the sofa, facing downstage towards an invisible black and white television set. They are watching in the dark, with just the ghostly television light upon them.

(Muted sounds of an old horror movie on the invisible television set from time to time. What they are watching is a very old, early thirties horror movie. MEREDITH *is cuddled under* JIM*'s arm. It's late at night. She's babysitting. She's eating a peach.)*

MEREDITH. Isn't this a great movie?

JIM. Are you kidding? This is the stupidest thing I've ever seen in my life. The people who aren't playing zombies are so bad they're more like zombies than the people playing zombies.

MEREDITH. It's remarkable how potent cheap music can be.

JIM. What?

MEREDITH. Noel Coward said that on the radio. He means that sometimes something that isn't actually made very well can still give you a lot of pleasure by creating a really powerful atmosphere you can get lost in.

JIM. I don't want to get lost. I want to watch something that makes sense, like football. Do you have to eat that damned peach? It's dripping all over the place. We've got popcorn and you're eating a peach.

MEREDITH. I was hungry for peaches. I've been getting all kinds of weird cravings lately. And sometimes I can smell bacon frying when nobody is cooking bacon. And also I've been hearing these radio broadcasts in my head. I mean, not real ones. It's like, there's this special frequency and I'm the only one tuned to it, and I can hear these voices and sounds and this music. It's just like murmuring in the background all the time, and sometimes somebody turns it up, and I can hear parts of it really clearly, and then it gets all garbled again.

JIM. What is it? Like Mars communicating with you? Is the mother ship calling you home?

MEREDITH. I don't think it's from Mars. I don't know where it's from. And I've been having a lot of nightmares, really disturbing ones, and I wake up in the middle of the night all sweaty and shaking so I go downstairs and open the refrigerator in the dark, because I like to see the light streaming out of the refrigerator into the darkness, like a picture of God in my old Bible story book.

JIM. So you've been hearing voices and smelling bacon and you think God lives in your refrigerator?

MEREDITH. No, silly. Not just my refrigerator. Everybody's refrigerator. I mean, if God is everywhere, then he's in the refrigerator, right?

JIM. You think he's in the toilet, too?

MEREDITH. I think everywhere means everywhere. If you believe that sort of thing. I don't know if I do or not. But I keep getting this feeling there's things going on all around me that I don't quite understand. It's like I'm a radio and my reception isn't good enough to draw in everything that's zapping through the air, so I just get these fragments of dialogue, sudden bursts of revelation, like listening to the radio late at night. Which I do sometimes when I can't sleep and go downstairs and have an onion and anchovy sandwich at three in the morning, and maybe I don't want to go back to sleep, because I've been dreaming that rats are eating the baby or something. And also I keep losing everything. I lost my keys. I lost my driver's license. I lost the cat. Except that came back. I lost my virginity in the back seat of your Chevy during *The Creature From The Black Lagoon* at the Drive-In. That's not coming back. Some things you can find again and some things, once you lose them, they're gone forever. And that's a long time. As we learn from popular songs on the radio. Also, I believe in ghosts.

JIM. There aren't any ghosts. That's almost as stupid as zombies.

MEREDITH. Well, it's not like Caspar the Friendly Ghost or people wearing sheets like in Three Stooges movies or anything like that. I mean I can feel these presences all around me. Like watching us.

JIM. Were they watching what we just did on the sofa?

MEREDITH. God, I hope not. Don't you ever get the feeling there's all kinds of presences around you, watching you?

JIM. No.

MEREDITH. You know why I liked you at first? Because you were so quiet. I figured that meant you were deep. But it turned out you just didn't have anything to say.

JIM. I've got plenty to say. I just don't feel like yapping all the time like you. Do they have any more beer?

MEREDITH. We can't drink all of Mr Palestrina's beer. I'm the babysitter. I can't get drunk.

JIM. But you can screw me on the sofa.

MEREDITH. Oh, God, we shouldn't have done that. What if Ben came down and saw us? What if he heard something and came down the steps and was looking at us from the doorway while it was happening?

JIM. Then he's a pervert.

MEREDITH. He's not a pervert. He's a little boy.

JIM. He's weird.

MEREDITH. He's not weird. Well, he's a little bit weird. But I like it. He's a lot nicer to me than you are.

JIM. He just wants to see you naked.

MEREDITH. He's five years old.

JIM. I've seen the way that kid looks at you in your swimsuit. Trust me, he wants to see you naked.

MEREDITH. But you like children, right?

JIM. No, I don't. They're a pain in the ass.

MEREDITH. You wouldn't like to have children some day?

JIM. Nope.

MEREDITH. But you would, if we got married.

JIM. I don't want to get married.

MEREDITH. You mean right now, or ever? You don't want to be alone for the rest of your life.

JIM. I'm not alone. You're here. Well, part of you is here. Most of you is usually someplace else, listening to the damned radio in your head.

MEREDITH. I'm not someplace else. Except sometimes I can almost remember being someplace else. Somebody else. Like before I was born.

JIM. What a bunch of crap that is.

MEREDITH. It's not crap. Ben told me he can almost remember being somebody else, in a previous life.

JIM. Ben is nuts, and so are you. You are the weirdest girl in this whole town. And this is a pretty weird town.

MEREDITH. I think you'd be good with children, if you had one. I mean, if we got married and had one.

JIM. If we got married and had a kid I'd step in front of the nearest locomotive.

MEREDITH. You don't mean that.

JIM. How do you know what I mean?

MEREDITH. It could happen, you know. Girls do get pregnant. And then what can you do?

JIM. Hop on the next boxcar to Fresno.

MEREDITH. You wouldn't do that.

JIM. I'd rather be dead. Like those zombies in this stupid movie.

(Pause. Sound of the movie.)

MEREDITH. Do you think zombies eat babies?

JIM. I don't know what zombies eat. I got to go. Me and Cletis are going hunting tomorrow.

MEREDITH. I don't understand how you can take pleasure from killing things.

JIM. It's human nature. Kill or be killed. Law of the Jungle. Ask the voices you hear on the radio in your head. They'll tell you.

MEREDITH. I don't like killing things.

> *(Pause.)*

Some people get rid of their babies before they're born. But I would never do that. I'd rather die.

JIM. *(Getting up and starting to go.)* Okay. See you later.

MEREDITH. *(Trying to pull him back.)* Wait. Don't you want to see the end of the movie?

JIM. I know the end of the movie. They kill the zombies. That's the end of the movie.

MEREDITH. Poor zombies. I feel sorry for them.

JIM. You feel sorry for zombies?

MEREDITH. Zombies are people, too.

JIM. You feel sorry for everything. You feel sorry for the chicken while you're eating it. You even felt sorry for the damned Creature From The Black Lagoon. All the time we were doing it in the back seat you were crying.

MEREDITH. Well, he was lonely.

JIM. He was a monster.

MEREDITH. He was just different. It's not a crime to be different. Or at least it shouldn't be.

JIM. Great. That's your perfect mate. Something with flippers and gills. You can have babies with him. Little frog face babies. I hope you'll be very happy together.

MEREDITH. I want to tell you something.

JIM. Tell me later.

MEREDITH. I could be dead later.

JIM. Then you can come back as a zombie and tell me while you're eating the baby.

> *(He goes. Pause.)*

MEREDITH. Yeah. Thanks a lot, Jim. You're a great listener. You're going to make a wonderful father some day.

(Pause. She sits down, looks at the movie.)

Watch out, zombies. They're coming to get you. I wonder if zombies hear voices in their heads. I bet they do. They always look like they're listening to something we can't hear. Maybe it's better to be dead. Or live at the bottom of a lagoon.

(Pause. Faint sound of the movie. She's listening to something else.)

What? Speak up. I can almost make it out. Like somebody is trying to tell me something. What are you trying to tell me? What should I do? Tell me what to do. Please tell me what to do.

(Sound of a faint screaming from inside the television set. The light fades on her and goes out.)

www.ingramcontent.com/pod-product-compliance
Lightning Source LLC
Chambersburg PA
CBHW072338300426
44109CB00042B/1738